COUCH TALES

COUCH TALES
Short Stories

by
Roger Kennedy

KARNAC

First published in 2009 by
Karnac Books Ltd
118 Finchley Road, London NW3 5HT

British Library Cataloguing in Publication Data
A C.I.P. for this book is available from the British Library

ISBN-13: 978-1-85575-569-7

Printed in Great Britain

www.karnacbooks.com

CONTENTS

PROLOGUE

I have a few minutes before my next patient. I have recently felt rather troubled about myself. I feel more and more muddled, though I do my work reasonably well. I suppose that sounds defensive. Rather typically for a man, I like to think that I do a good job; and I like to tell people I do, maybe because I am not convinced myself. I do not think it is the same for women; that is to say, they assume you know that they are capable, once you get to know them as people. Maybe that's too sweeping an assertion.

This relationship business is becoming more and more of a puzzle to me. Perhaps that is why I have suddenly had the idea of writing down a few short stories, based loosely on my work, and focusing on different aspects of relationships. Being an analyst, it would not be surprising if I highlighted the more unusual, even perverse, areas of emotional life. I do not necessarily mean to imply that we are all completely fucked up; although sometimes I do wonder how on earth we survive, given our remarkable capacity to hurt one another.

Most of my working life consists of listening to stories, albeit of a particular kind, often with little structure and with many different narrative threads or "voices." It often feels like being in a maze, as there are so many ways of interpreting what I hear. With so many different voices to take in, you have to follow your gut feelings and come to where you think the heart of the matter lies. At times, you just have to let the patient have their say and tell their story in their own way and at their own speed.

I do not intend to make my stories into clinical accounts. I shall describe various characters' life stories, based loosely on their analysis with me, on our mutual encounter. I hope that I am not abusing my position. *My patients come to me to be understood, not for other people's entertainment. So I shall heavily disguise their identity and mix in elements from my own life, which is full of failings and defects. I hope I hardly have to emphasise that analysts are not paragons of virtue, although our patients frequently wish we were. We are fallible, pathetic and, in some ways, socially crippled. After all, we spend all day virtually immobile, while not having real or ordinary relationships with our patients. Our abstention, though no doubt noble, has a price—that we can often forget what the real world gets up to. By the way, I am not going to get into the issue of whether or not analysis is effective; that would take me away from my current task of producing fiction. Mind you, the detractors of psychoanalysis consider it a fiction anyway, of course.

My next patient is late. I have the opportunity to write down a few more thoughts. It is very decent of him to give me more time to myself. Now this is where I bring in the personal contribution. I have to admit that things have not been too easy at home recently. Kathy, my wife, has been under considerable stress at work and this has begun to affect our relationship. We have less and less time with one another, and I spend more and more time on my own. Perhaps that is why the idea of the stories arose, in order to fill some sort of space in my life. Otherwise time would hang heavy on me.

I hope that this is a temporary situation, and that I just have to stick things out. She is a capable professional, a paediatrician at a London teaching hospital. Her department might be closed or merged with another hospital, and she might lose her job, or lose her team. It is a very difficult situation to have to cope with. She has

*The author wishes to make clear that in fact none of the stories are based upon real patients, and also that the psychoanalyst of the book is fictitious.

to spend extra time away from home dealing with all the politics. I quite understand the stress it causes her—the job itself is stressful enough, without additional burdens. Unfortunately, there does not seem to be much that I can do to help, except to be available to her. What is worrying is that our two children are beginning to complain that she is not around enough. At least I work at home and can be around from time to time. Do I detect a note of bitterness in my jottings? Resentment, certainly. Where is this all leading me?

I should add that the idea for these stories came to me while I was attending a regular meeting of colleagues. We get together to discuss our work in a supportive atmosphere. It struck me that we are constantly presenting stories, however much we dress them up in analytic jargon. I even had the thought that I should make up a story and present it to them as if it were a case history to see how they would respond, and whether or not they would pick up that it was a fiction. But I resisted the idea, probably out of fear that they would not take me seriously as an analyst. More insecurity…

I have already worked out the plot of the first story. It came to me all of a sudden in the middle of a session, during a long silence. I have begun to jot down ideas for other stories in a little notebook I carry with me. I feel that there is somehow going to be a thread running through the project. But I am deeply suspicious of writing that aims merely to be therapeutic for the writer, as it veers towards the self-indulgent. In order to guard against that temptation I shall make some comments about each story in a journal, as I go along. Yet, knowing me, something else may well intrude. I cannot refrain from allowing my thoughts to arise from wherever it is they come from, and letting them rove wherever it is they wish to go. An occupational disease, you might say.

The bell has rung. The patient has arrived. The work begins.

Mr Samson, or the game of love

Mr Samson was in his late thirties. That is not his real name, but I think it sums him up succinctly, for he is well built, physically powerful, but also emotionally vulnerable. Furthermore, he would be quite capable of bringing down his own house on top of himself, let alone the palace of the Philistines.

To look at him, you feel that his emotions are only just held in check, and that there is a boiler inside him about to explode beneath his powerful frame. Indeed, beneath his veneer of intellectual sophistication he is full of self-loathing and doubt. Nonetheless, he has a considerable presence, even charisma. He has a large brow, a beautiful aquiline nose and sensuous lips. The combination of physical strength and gentleness in manner produce a charming effect; however, at times his intellectual power and learning can be formidable. It can arouse considerable envy among his colleagues in the university department where he lectures on cultural studies and psychoanalysis. On the other hand, he has quite a following among the students and is a popular teacher. I should say that it was interest in psychoanalysis that propelled him into treatment, and not the other way round. I should also add that he knows more about the theory of analysis

1

than I do. He is always presenting on psychoanalysis, politics and linguistics at seminars and conferences.

Despite his professional accomplishments, he is not a worldly man. Not that he is naive or innocent, he just does not care much for material possessions. His flat is always knee-deep in books and papers, and he cares little for money. However, he once had the opportunity to live well and comfortably, since his wife, whom he married in his early twenties, came from an old, established and wealthy family of merchant bankers. They took him into their hearts and pockets, and offered him all sorts of financial rewards for the privilege of being allied to their stock, not to mention their shares.

At first, he revelled in the situation. He had come from a poor family of limited education and had yet managed to get to grammar school and then university. Never before had he been so intimate with the well-to-do. There was a limitless supply of books. These people gave as much thought to the price of things as the air they breathed.

His wife, Emily, was pleasant enough, a kind if somewhat suppressed, tight-lipped young woman, whom he had met at university. She found him thrilling, particularly as he was so unlike all her rather superficial friends and especially her stuffy family. They lived a life of ease in a flat bought by her parents, while he completed his doctoral thesis. She made plans for their future; he was too busy with his studies to think beyond the next page of references. He felt reasonably content, if a little under-stimulated, and followed her plans, even if half-heartedly. It was as if they were characters in a dream, caught up in their own story but fleeting and fragile, liable to dissolve at any moment. Perhaps there was too much comfort and not enough stark reality. They certainly had none of the material struggles of most young couples, which, after all, can cement a relationship, provided the stresses are not too great. They were united by the illusion of contentment, which soon began to fade.

It was difficult to know when it began to go wrong, but the final rupture came one Sunday lunchtime at her family's mansion in Kensington. They had reached the main course when Mr Samson perceived his surroundings as if he had woken up to a room full of strangers. His father-in-law was a tall, lean, quietly spoken man who hardly moved his lips when speaking, as if he were his own ventriloquist. He was carving the joint slowly and carefully with great concentration. His wife, meanwhile, was engaged in conversation with Mr Samson. She was a nervy, fidgety woman, unable to tolerate silence and prone to sudden fits of extreme fatigue. She was wound up and stressed, like a taut string about to break. They were discussing a recent Surrealist exhibition at the Hayward Gallery—she liked to play the art lover with him. It was certainly easier for her than discussing his work, which even then concerned psychoanalysis, for she had a loathing of anything that smacked of psychology; indeed, introspection produced in her extreme nausea.

"I do love Dali's drooping clocks, don't you?" she said, pressing his arm.

"I'm not sure," he replied awkwardly and suppressing a desire to brush her hand away, as if it were an irritating wasp.

"I think he is so fascinating."

"He's a bit too glib for me," he finally replied. "What did Freud say about Dali? Ah, yes—too conscious, not enough unconscious."

"Oh, really?" she said, somewhat mystified but also thrilled, for she loved his unusual vision of things. It was more interesting than being in conversation with her bony husband, who was painfully intent on never having a difference of opinion on anything.

She was still holding onto Mr Samson as he reached out to sip his glass of wine. As she let go of him, she continued, "The whole experience was so liberating, don't you think?"

"Yes, I suppose it was," he replied dryly.

"Is that enough meat, dear?" her husband asked.

"Oh, yes, yes," she replied impatiently.

"I bought one of those surreal sort of things," her husband said to the air. "A couple of years ago. Rather intrigued me. Can't think who the artist was. Who was he, dear?" he asked deferentially of his wife.

"You mean the one with the funny forest shapes?" she said, screwing up her dry face. "In the hall?"

"Max Ernst," said Mr Samson curtly.

"Oh, yes, of course," she said.

"The German fellow?" said her husband.

"Swiss," said Mr Samson.

"Ah," replied the husband meaningfully to himself. "More meat?" he then asked, turning to Mr Samson.

The latter's wife, a plump, serious young woman, who looked up to him as an oracle, noticed that he was seething with rage.

But as usual in her parents' house, she fell mute. She bore his irritation with a sickly smile, which only enhanced his sense of alienation.

But suddenly Mr Samson became calm. His anger dispersed and he felt almost regal, with a sense of his own superiority. The barrier between them, which before had felt like a terrible chasm, was now a cause for celebration. His expression changed from the habitual strained one that he usually assumed in their company into one of serenity, even a kind of beatitude. His hosts noticed this change and assumed that he was at last happy in their presence. His wife almost burst into tears with relief. Although she had married him as a sort of rebellion against her family's values, she could not bear the tension when there was a clash of values over Sunday lunch.

The dessert, apple crumble with double cream, was the moment of crisis. He excused himself, ostensibly to go to the toilet, but instead he left the house, his wife, her family, and a life of ease. He could not stomach them any more. The double cream was the last straw. It just seemed too rich for his taste.

To his relief, but also slight chagrin, his wife, though initially distraught over his leaving, did little to persuade him to return, no doubt influenced by her parents. After arranging for his many books to be collected, they spoke once more and then never again.

After an unsettled period living in various flats and rooms, during which, however, he completed his thesis and gained a lecturing post, he met his second wife, Jane, a very bright but brittle literature graduate. They shared a common disinterest in worldly possessions except books, which were scattered throughout their flat. Cooking was a joint activity, or rather a joint scattering of objects from the kitchen to the dining table. They made a good intellectual team, but were emotionally precarious, both singly and together. Their moods affected each other adversely, so that while one was up the other was down; which meant that they felt unable to make consistent emotional contact with one another. Perhaps that was why children were never on the agenda. Her doctorate continued to remain unfinished for a few years while she worked on various sources and letters. During this time, their relationship, though at times strained, held together.

However, at some point the precarious balance of the marriage was upset. He cited two factors. The first was that at last she had begun, with his help, to collect together the various fragments of her work into a coherent whole. Far from being a relief, the possibility of accomplishing this task successfully made her very anxious. She became sensitive to noise, afraid that objects might break, and even anxious about cracking open an egg, as the fragments terrified her. Yet at the same time, the work proceeded satisfactorily.

The other factor which tipped them over the edge was an affair she began with a research psychologist at a weekend conference. She became quite obsessed with him, much to his amusement and then embarrassment. During this conference she would not leave his side and was openly flirtatious. Afterwards, she plagued him with telephone calls. The infatuation soon passed, but then she threw herself at other men quite indiscriminately, and unfairly taunted Mr Samson with their sexual prowess and his lack of manliness.

The situation reached breaking point when Jane brought a man back to their flat and openly flaunted herself before Mr Samson. There was a scene, after which she ran off, leaving the men to sort out the situation, which they did fairly amicably.

In the weeks that followed, Mr Samson had no news of Jane. Rather as he had walked out on his first wife for good and with no intention of meeting her again, Jane had done the same to him. He became increasingly filled with loneliness and despair. He hardly ate or slept. He would spend hours at night looking out of his flat in the hope that she would return. Recalling what he had done to his first wife, he had bouts of remorse; he even thought of contacting her again, but thought better of it—for all he knew, she had remarried and he could not face further rejection.

He began to deteriorate physically and mentally. He lost weight and looked ill, with a haunted expression on his sallow face. He would roam the streets at night on the look-out for Jane, staring at passers by, who took him for a vagrant. On one of these desperate journeys, he found himself wandering into a neighbouring house which he knew from rumour to be a brothel, with the intention of relieving his frustration. The place had a minimum of decor and smelled of damp, which hardly added to its allure. But he was greeted by a friendly, fat, middle-aged lady who put him at ease. She led him into a lounge where several girls were smoking and chatting, in various states of undress. He picked a girl at random and she led him up a flight of stairs into a room, bare save for a double bed, a couple of chairs and a sink.

She was kind to him, if lacking passion; and, to his surprise, the act gave him much pleasure. He had been led to believe that sex with a prostitute was a heartless affair, lacking in human warmth. Perhaps it was a measure of his desperation that he was so taken by the experience. Whatever the reason, he was grateful to her.

He returned to her on several occasions. Gradually, he began to know her better and to take an interest in her. She, in turn, seemed to like his company and would allow him more time than usual for his money. She called herself Lisa and came from a town in the Yorkshire Dales. She was in her early twenties, quite pretty, with a slim figure and a warm, round face. He liked the fact that she did not wear heavy make-up, like the others, and he liked her smell of lavender.

Apparently, she had always been a handful at home, rebellious and headstrong. Her parents had divorced when she was a baby, while her stepfather had treated her badly. She left home to escape his attacks when she was sixteen, and came down to London, where she gradually drifted into her current lifestyle. She once sent her family a card, but they did not reply and then they had lost contact. He was sympathetic to her story, for they had both walked out of a family and had been abandoned in turn. This gave them a special understanding and a sort of intimacy. She talked freely to him and he respected her openness. There was, ironically, an absence of hypocrisy in her pretence at being intimate. It was like playing a game.

He surprised himself one evening after a session by having the thought that he loved Lisa. It was ridiculous, for he was only one of many clients. Yet in a sense that only increased his fervour, for he imagined that he was her favourite, the special client, who understood her and cared for her.

At first, he kept his thoughts secret, for he imagined that she would be frightened by any declaration of love. It might push the boundaries of their relationship too far and into dangerous territory. She might even refuse to see him again, and that would be disastrous, for he did not want to spoil his new-found confidence. As a result of his encounters with her, he had managed to feel whole again. His appearance returned to normal and he began to forget Jane, whom he found out was living with another lecturer.

However, his feelings came out at the climax of a session, as he came into Lisa and shouted out that he loved her. As they disengaged, he could hardly look at her lest she were disgusted by his declaration. In fact, she either did not notice or was unconcerned. When he repeated the declaration the next time, with the same result, he plucked up courage to ask her whether or not she was insulted by his feelings. She replied that, on the contrary, she was flattered by them, but it was clear from the way that she answered him that their relationship remained on a professional basis.

He then came up with the notion that they might pretend to be lovers, as part of a sexual fantasy. That way, he could obtain what he desired, and she would understand that the fantasy would be kept within the bounds of the room. He came to her every night, sometimes with presents, always with affection. He covered her with kisses, which she accepted. He wrote her a poem, which she kept.

However, one night, some six months after they met, she disappeared from the brothel. The Madame did not know where she had gone; it was common enough for girls to come and go. He refused a substitute, however alluring, and walked back to his flat, utterly devastated. He briefly thought of suicide, but soon pulled himself round. After all, Lisa, or whoever she really was, had never promised him more than her paid time. She had walked out, but then such exits had become familiar to him now; they no longer took him by surprise. He only regretted that he had no photograph of her to remember her by. She was the love of his life. Who is to tell whether or not this form of love is more or less worthy that other forms? At least it gave him enormous satisfaction. He did not repeat his fantasy with other prostitutes, but remained faithful to Lisa. He cherished her image and the good time they had had together. He became a much happier man.

Journal

I suppose that there was a sort of irony running through Mr Samson's life, in that his search for intimacy could only be achieved through a game or a fantasy. But what is genuine love, and who is to determine what it is? Even Freud pointed out that the love of a patient for their analyst was as genuine as any other love. Analysts resemble prostitutes in taking payment for intimate services; although, of course, we do not necessarily promise satisfaction. Nor, hopefully, do we disappear without warning, though that is a common fear.

Mr Samson seemed fascinated by ideas. Even his love for Lisa was more the love for an idea rather than a reality. And yet ideas have started wars, written books, transformed lives, and made us love. We should not, then, have a narrow definition of love, nor a low estimate of the power of ideas to move us.

I wish I were satisfied with what I have. The happiness I find is never enough for me. The more I enjoy the moment, the more enjoyment I want in the future. Perhaps I am a little like Mr Samson, too distant and controlled as a person. Not that I have been with a prostitute. Despite my curiosity, I would be too afraid to try. I am one of those people who have to know someone before I can make love. Anonymity freezes me.

I feel guilty about retreating to my consulting room in order to type the stories on my laptop. I noticed some irritated looks from Kathy. In future I shall work early in the morning before the others are awake. I notice that I am trying to justify myself, trying to look good, as if I know that I am in the wrong.

Kathy said recently that we have become too comfortable. We are in our early forties and have become used to a quiet life—seeing friends, mainly couples, over dinner, or occasionally going out to the theatre or opera. Nothing too wild. Maybe she has a point. At least our sexual life is still pretty active. My desire for her has grown over the years. I have always been highly sexed. Typical male egoism. I thought she was happy with our life. I feel I am losing control. Is that a bad thing?

I have to admit that I do not like to hear what she has to say. I would rather things remain as they are. I like being comfortable. I like the certainty of knowing who is sleeping beside me. Something is up. Is she having an affair? Do I dare ask her? The trouble with questions is that they invite answers.

Perhaps I am letting my imagination run riot. It is all the fault of this story-telling business. You can start to believe in your own plots. My story is one of mid-life. It is a dangerous time, as we all know. A period of transition, change and crisis, of loss of youth, and the approach of death. One or two of your friends come down with serious illnesses, one may die of cancer; your parents weaken and become dependent on you for the first time; several couples divorce; your children approach adolescence and threaten to challenge your values; you may either work hard to keep fit and your body trim (like me) or you may give up the struggle and become flabby (my terror). For some it offers the chance of a new beginning, for others there is the prospect of unfulfilled ambitions.

Who the hell am I, anyway? I am forty-three years old, a happily married man with a delightful and clever son and daughter, nine and eleven respectively. I have an attractive and interesting wife whom I love dearly. It matters to me that she is attractive, and that other men are drawn to her. I freely admit this piece of male vanity. It gives me a buzz just to look at her. What can possibly be wrong with our life? We have had thirteen happy years together. And yet, if I am honest, Kathy seems to be unhappy with the way we are now, though she never used to be. Is it always women who determine where a relationship should go? Are they the real pace-setters? Her changed attitude fills me with anxiety. I suppose I can tell myself that she is merely under stress from her work and not from me and that the crisis, if there is one, will soon pass.

Mind you, I have sometimes had the thought, just before reaching home, that I might enter the house to find some disaster greeting me, that one of the children has died or that Kathy has left. I trust her absolutely—well, almost—but there is still the occasional fear that she has tired of me.

Occasional has now become frequent. Yes, it is true. Why deny it? Why can't I talk to her about my fears? Would that make them go away, or implant more doubts in her mind? A dilemma.

We seem to have been together for so long that perhaps I have taken her for granted, and vice versa. Maybe a bit of distance would not be a bad thing. Of course, I could have an affair. Men are prone to use their cocks when anxious about their age, their women, and their fragile egos. But just thinking about it frightens me. I no longer relish the seduction process. It just seems such an effort. But suppose the opportunity came my way? There have been a number of occasions when I could have grasped the nettle. I do have a position of some authority in my field, and am aware that this is attractive to some women. Until now, I have been determined to behave myself; I have thought the mess and the complications not worth the effort. But it would certainly have an impact on Kathy. Why not admit that I want to get at her? Yet there are the children to think about. Still, there is no harm in fantasising, is there? It is like thinking up stories.

I have an elderly patient who likes telling me long stories about his life. One in particular grabbed my interest, and I shall tell it in his own words. It deeply affected his life; indeed, the pain it caused never left him.

Three and a Bomber

It was a long time ago, when I was a raw youth. Don't laugh, I was young once. I wasn't always such an old fogey. It was in the war, when I was a navigator in Bomber Command. Actually, most of the best stories in Bomber Command cannot be told as the chaps died on the job. We had a high death rate—it must have been only a one in ten chance of survival, and we were all volunteers. Crazy to think about it now. It is hard to think of myself as a brave young warrior now that I am a grandfather.

Try to imagine what it was like—going up in the air not knowing whether you would return to base alive. There were seven in a crew: the pilot or captain, navigator, flight engineer, wireless operator, bomb aimer and front-gunner, mid-upper, and rear gunners. I had a little curtained-off compartment in our Lancaster where I did my calculations. At times it got quite hair-raising. Can you imagine trying to calculate your position when there is a German fighter sweeping in on you? Of course, most of us were barely out of adolescence, and, though we were afraid, it was also an adventure. It gave you a buzz being a hero, doing your bit to beat the Jerries. There was also the camaraderie on the ground and in the air, in your own crew and between crews. I have never

11

experienced anything as intense or as pleasurable since, as the bond between us in the squadron.

Don't laugh now—they were good chaps, all of them. Mind you, if we had really known what we were doing to the Germans beneath us, I am not sure what we would have done. But we hardly thought of them as people. It was war and we just had to bomb the enemy and do as much damage as possible. In fact, half the time we didn't know what we were doing. We certainly didn't hit the targets regularly. Instead, we just sprayed the ground with masses of bombs and hoped for the best, or the worst. Sometimes you were afraid that your own planes might drop their bombs on you, if you happened to get beneath them. It could be very confusing in the air, especially if you had to take action to avoid enemy fighters.

We lived for the moment and cherished our friendships while they lasted. I suppose it made us an effective fighting team, though I think it was mainly our way of coping with the anxiety of it all.

Though we went through many dangerous situations, something more personal happened to us that turned out to be, in a sense, even more dangerous to us. I have certainly never forgotten the events, even though I can barely recall all the raids we made. It involved a couple of my close mates, the rear gunner and the pilot, and of course a girl was involved.

Sandy, our pilot and captain, was a tall, fair, handsome young man, with a natural sense of authority. We followed his instructions without question. He took us in and out of many raids with hardly a scratch on the plane. In time, we began to believe we led a charmed life thanks to him. Sandy himself shrugged this off as nonsense. Though the son of a parson, we was irreligious, irreverent, and a materialist. He was openly proud of his rampant atheism, despite the ubiquitous presence of death. In the air, he was a professional to the core. With fierce concentration he would focus on the task at hand, so that we all felt secure, despite the barrage of anti-aircraft fire. On the ground, he let it all hang out, as they say nowadays. Off duty, he loved a drink or two or three and was often pretty drunk, although he could sober up remarkably quickly. Whenever there was a spare moment, he was usually to be found at the mess bar fondling a drink. He enjoyed a song, for he had a passable tenor voice, and he liked women and chased after them when the opportunity arose.

My other mate, Jim, the rear gunner, was a very different character. He was a quiet and unassuming man, self-contained and thoughtful, even something of a philosopher. He could brood for hours over some weighty problem, and he had definite views about what we were doing. He was clear about the need to make war against the enemy, but he thought we were bombing too heavily. I suppose the rest of us just accepted our lot and got on with our duty. We were too young and inexperienced in life to do otherwise. I still do not know whether or not we did the right thing by using saturation bombing, and whether or not it helped bring the war to an end sooner.

In the air, Jim was devoted to the task at hand and was a very effective gunner. Indeed, he came to life behind the gun. He loved shooting at enemy fighters and was ecstatic if he ever hit one. But when we were out of danger, he would return to being taciturn; perhaps he regretted the pleasure of the kill.

Now, Sandy and Jim became attached to the same woman, and that was the trouble I was referring to. It began when we were out on the town, living it up after a bout of heavy raids inside Germany. Several of us from the squadron found ourselves in the same dance hall eager to have a good time with some girls. Sandy was a great dancer. He charmed women with his boyish sense of fun and, thanks to him, we were soon surrounded by a group of girls who were fascinated by our uniforms and the risks we took, which of course we played up like mad.

As the evening wore on, we found ourselves paired up. We danced and kissed a lot, occasionally coming together for a drink and a laugh. But, somehow, Sandy and Jim were with the same dark-haired girl, Dawn, a nurse. I think Jim found her first, but then Sandy asked her to dance, and then Jim stuck with her rather than find another partner. She was vivacious, often with a wicked smile on her lively face, as if about to do something incredibly naughty, or as if she had just done it and did not care a damn.

There was no obvious tension between the three of them that night. Sandy would make the other two laugh, while Jim would make the occasional ironic comment. They took turns to dance with Dawn, who was flattered by the double ration of attention. Soon, they seemed to create a world of their own, separate from the rest of us. This felt strange at first as we were used to having

Sandy at the centre of things. Yet for once he appeared to enjoy being apart from us. Jim was used to being on the margins. He saw himself as different from the rest. Though we quite liked him and he was part of the team, he set himself up as a kind of observer or commentator on what we were doing, a sort of Greek chorus, and that irritated us.

At a certain point, we noticed that the three had slipped out. When we saw Sandy and Jim the next morning, they looked solemn and preoccupied. They would not tell us what had happened. While the rest of us were lively and full of sparkle, despite some hangovers, they looked funereal. Soon their black mood descended on us all, and there were only a few subdued whispers. We guessed what had happened, though it was only later that I found out that the three had indeed slept together. The men regretted the experience, which they found disturbing, though Dawn had apparently enjoyed it. Later on in the trio's relationship, the men tended to take it in turns with her on a rota basis, though she occasionally insisted they do it all together.

Sandy and Jim cheered up once we returned to action in the sky, but our luck there seemed to change. We were hit badly by anti-aircraft fire while part of a massive raid over Cologne, and were unable to discharge our bombs on target. We limped back to base on two of our four engines, and the plane had to undergo major repairs. We hoped for an extended leave, but of course we were provided with another plane. A major bombing offensive was just beginning and they wanted every available crew in action. There was a general feeling that the Germans were on the run and we were not to let them off the hook. I think that this was around the time of their retreat from Stalingrad.

At first, none of the crew spoke about our recent misfortune. However, it was Jim who spoke for us all when he said that our luck had changed, and that he felt partly responsible. Sandy tried to take all the blame himself. The rest us insisted that it was no one's fault, and that it had been nothing short of miraculous that we had escaped damage until then. Yet, however rational we tried to remain, deep inside us we felt that Sandy's charmed life had deserted him and us. It is difficult to know what gives groups confidence. Perhaps it grows when trust develops between you and gives you a sense of belonging. Once our plane was changed, it was as if we had also changed, and the group began to feel weaker. I began to have bad dreams and to feel cold and lonely in bed.

In addition, Dawn had a bad effect on us all. Whenever we had any free time she was always tagging along, accompanying Sandy and Jim. Though we could not help but find her physically attractive, we became increasingly suspicious of her. Maybe we would have felt the same about any woman coming too close to any of us. Speaking for myself, I only wanted a good time with a girl, partly because of my youth, but also because I did not know how long I would survive. Dawn's continued presence paradoxically brought us up against the threat to our lives by reminding us of the possibility of a lasting relationship.

Gradually, we found ourselves becoming irritable with one another, which was disastrous for our morale. We had come through countless missions night and day, often in the early days with hardly any fighter escort, buoyed by our confidence and good morale. Mind you, much of Bomber Command was the same. Despite the casualties, or perhaps because of them, we were determined to fight on. I suppose we felt that we were really getting at Hitler personally, for we were striking directly at the Germans, behind their lines. Look, I don't want to blame Dawn for what happened. All three were to blame, plus the desperation of war. Wherever you looked, people were at it, trying to have a good time, trying to live a whole life in a few days.

Jim wrote almost daily letters to Dawn, while Sandy never wrote one. While the rest of us would chat endlessly about our brief encounters and hopeless longings, Sandy and Jim remained silent. I later discovered that there had initially been a bit of a fight for Dawn's attentions. After that first night, when they had all slept together, the men decided to avoid a repeat of the situation if possible. So they put it to her to choose one of them. But she was unable to make up her mind as she hardly knew either of them. It was a shame that the lads did not call off the affair there and then; but obviously something powerful led them on, until they became so involved and entangled with one another that retreat was impossible.

While Dawn was supposedly making up her mind, she spent time with each of them in turn, in order to obtain a better picture of their different qualities. The problem was that, in her eyes, both of them were incomplete as individuals. Sandy was charming but not as deep as Jim. Jim was thoughtful but not as exciting as Sandy. Sandy was good at seduction, but Jim was a more capable lover, a better performer. Sandy was good at exciting her interest, while Jim was better at fulfilling it. When she was with one of them, she missed the other.

Of the men, Sandy most disliked the arrangement, for he naturally assumed that Dawn would prefer him. Though he found the whole situation infuriating, he was unable to extricate himself from the triangle. To some extent, the situation represented a challenge to him. Used to easy success with women, he was puzzled by having to share favours. He saw the conquering of Dawn as another kind of battle.

Jim, on the other hand, seemed happy enough with the arrangement. He had access to an attractive woman, and yet was not fully committed to her because of Sandy. He did not mind sharing her. However, Sandy was tormented by the thought of Jim making love to Dawn. He kept imagining the two of them in bed together when he himself made love to her. The other man's presence was always before him, interfering with his pleasure, as if someone had rifled through his belongings. Jim, on the contrary, found Sandy's involvement an added excitement. He was aroused by the knowledge that another man had recently entered Dawn's body. The fact that this man was someone he liked and admired only increased his enjoyment.

Of course, their affair carried on only in brief moments of leave after a series of missions. The actual time they spent together was minimal; but they were living in another kind of time, a personal time that had its own strange laws.

The stage was soon passed when she was expected to make a choice between them; indeed, the subject was dropped. Clearly, she had chosen to keep both men, which pleased Jim but annoyed Sandy. The latter asserted that he would have preferred a clear rejection, but he did nothing to remove himself from the situation. I think he was genuinely fond of Dawn and maybe even loved her. He did try a couple of flings with other girls while Jim was with Dawn, but they always disappointed him. Perhaps he accepted the *ménage* because of the intense war conditions. Everything at that time was both intensely exhilarating and unreal. We lived in an enclosed world, cooped up with men, often with little sleep and intent on doing damage to the enemy. We could not afford to let our spirits flag too much, and anyway we were buoyed by the other men. To compensate for the absence of women, we named aircraft after them and spent many waking hours fantasising about them. Occasionally, we wondered whether we would spend the best years of our youth perpetually dropping bombs, and feared that we might have to bale out and spend the war in a P.O.W. camp, with no prospect of seeing women. We had to grow up quickly in order to take on adult responsibilities. We had to face danger like men, though emotionally we were still boys. We had to make love when we could, throwing caution to the winds.

Sandy tried unsuccessfully to forget that Jim was his co-partner in love. Instead, he tried to view him in a military context as a member of his battle team. Sandy found this approach more acceptable, for in that way they were sort of engaged in a combined operation. In addition, Sandy could remind himself that Jim was a subordinate, both in bed and in the Lancaster. Indeed, there was a kind of similarity in Jim's role in both places, for he was aggressive in the rear turret and potent between the sheets. But he lacked tenderness, which Sandy possessed. Sandy's concern for the crew made us feel secure. He could be a bastard when necessary, especially if there was any sloppy preparation; but he was concerned for our welfare and made himself available to listen to our views and worries. Despite his youth, he was like a father to us.

No doubt Dawn found this aspect of his personality irresistible, but clearly it was not enough to command her undivided interest. The rest of us knew what was going on, but preferred to keep off the subject—until one night, just before a raid, when Sandy became drunk, which was in his own eyes an unpardonable sin. He had ploughed his way through a whole bottle of cheap whisky. He became maudlin, moaning on about Dawn and his sorry plight. If the senior officers had seen his state he would have been in deep trouble. So we bundled him off to our quarters, poured black coffee down his throat and sprayed him with cold water. Eventually he sobered up enough to bluff his way through the briefing. But later he was mortified at his behaviour. In his own words, it was totally unprofessional and the greatest insult to the squadron. We did our best to cheer him up; it was the least we could do after all the support he had given us. But he could not forgive himself for having lost control.

It was then that some of us got to talking, as a result of which I was nominated to have a serious discussion with Jim about the situation. All our sympathies were now with Sandy, our captain, whom we did not like to see suffer, while Jim seemed untouched by the complexities of the *ménage*. We decided to interfere with their personal business because we judged that our lives were being put at risk by their behaviour.

Jim and I used to have occasional long "philosophical" chats into the night as we had both become insomniacs. So I was a natural choice to be the one to confront him. I scrounged a few cigarettes to use as sweeteners, and picked a moment when Jim and I were alone in our quarters.

"Well, Jim, looks like we're going over France soon," I said, offering him a cigarette, which he took in silence. "Help with the invasion."

"Hmm," he replied, apparently unconcerned about future missions and puffing away, self absorbed.

"Doesn't bother you?" I asked.

"Should it?"

"It's better than bombing cities."

"True," he acknowledged.

"More like a real battle."

"Yes." At last he looked me in the eye. "I'd feel better about that. Not that I care that much any more," he added with a sigh. "You become hardened."

"You don't sound too happy," I said, hoping to lead him on to talk about his love life.

"Who, me? I'm all right. Mustn't grumble, as they say. Got to keep up the jolly old morale," he said, with a cynical smile.

"I was just thinking about, er, you know," I said awkwardly, trying to get to the point.

"No."

"Sandy and you," I said at last.

"Oh, that," he replied, waiting for me to continue.

"Well, the lads were talking about it."

"Good for them."

"I know it's none of our business."

"Dead right."

"It wasn't our concern before. but it is now. Sandy is cracking up."

"I can't help that. It's not my fault. If you can't stand the heat, stay out of the kitchen."

"The problem is in the bedroom."

"What about it?" he said impatiently.

"Can't you resolve the situation? It's getting dangerous, with Sandy drunk."

"Not up to me," said Jim with a shrug.

"Why not?" I challenged, finding his stonewalling infuriating.

"If he wants to give her up, that's his business. I won't."

"Even if it kills us all?"

"Don't exaggerate."

"You could change crews."

"Maybe I could," he replied, somewhat hurt by my suggestion.

"We are behind the skipper, Jim. You should know that."

"Send me to Coventry, if you must."

"Don't be stupid. That's why I'm talking to you now, to see if you'll see sense."

"Look, it's Dawn's choice, not mine. She's happy enough, as far as I can tell."

"We're not. It's tearing us apart. You can cut the atmosphere with a knife."

"I hadn't noticed."

"That's just the trouble."

"Well, there's not a bloody thing I can do about it, mate," he retorted.

We stared at one another for a few moments. I imagined that I saw a flicker of desperation in his eyes. Perhaps he had become so hopelessly caught up in the love triangle that he really was unable to disentangle himself.

"Do you want any help, Jim?" I asked, trying to respond to his despair. He shrugged his shoulders and told me to piss off.

Having got nowhere with Jim, I took it on myself to have a chat with Sandy. Luckily, I found him sitting alone in the mess with a drink.

"Hello, old chap," he said eagerly. "Take a pew. What'll it be?" I took a pint of beer to his table.

"I hear it won't be long before we go to Normandy," I began, to make conversation.

"It's all the same to me," he replied, swilling down his beer.

"You all right now, Sandy?" I asked with concern.

"There's always a drink," he replied, finishing off his pint. He fetched another for both of us.

After a while, I plucked up courage to face him with our concerns.

"It's a rum business," he admitted. "Look," he continued, in a confidential whisper. "I don't know what to do. Jim has some power over Dawn so she won't let him go. I know he's one of us, one of the crew and all that, but he is eerie. Look, keep this under your belt. The other night, when we had leave, it was my turn with her. We were bonking away, when suddenly there was this crashing noise from her wardrobe. Don't laugh, it's true. I went over to the bloody thing, and bloody Jim was there, watching us at it. I was bloody angry, as you can imagine. We would have come to blows if Dawn weren't there. She didn't mind about it. The fellow likes watching, gives him a kick. Maybe her, too."

"Why don't you give her up?"

"I can't," he replied feebly. "I'm in love with her. Maybe I also feel sorry for her. She's had a difficult life. Poor home, lots of beatings, that sort of thing. I feel sort of protective."

"Well, Jim should be stopped," I said angrily.

"For all I know, the bastard's been watching all along."

"It's beyond me," I admitted. "The only thing, Sandy, is that it's putting us all at risk. We're beginning to doubt you, and that's disastrous for morale. Corrosive. I don't want to go up again. I've never really felt like that, not deep down."

He was silent for a while, contemplating what I had said.

"You're right," he said finally. "It's not on."

At that point we dropped the conversation as some other men appeared.

No more was said about the affair for some time. We began to raid Normandy, while Allied forces gradually drove back the Germans. We felt at last that we were going to win, though of course the Germans fought fiercely, and we were subjected to repeated fighter and anti-aircraft fire. Luckily, Jim and Sandy were at opposite ends of the plane, which seemed to keep the peace.

However, one evening we found them in our quarters shouting at each other. Jim was particularly furious, with his face almost red to bursting.

"Leave me alone!" Sandy shouted.

"No, I fucking won't!" Jim screamed. "You can't run out on us. I won't let you."

When we entered, Jim made for me, pushing his face right up against mine. "It's your bloody fault, you interfering prat!" he screamed again, spraying me with spit.

At first I was too shocked to respond. But when Sandy came to my rescue by putting himself between Jim and me, I came to my senses.

"It's alright, Sandy," I said, with growing anger. "I'll deal with him."

"It's not your quarrel," Sandy replied, still shielding me.

I stepped out from behind Sandy, and said with exasperation: "What the hell is going on?"

"This really is too much," said Sandy.

"I don't care who knows!" exclaimed Jim.

"Let's all calm down," I pleaded.

Eventually, the situation became clearer, if still confused. Jim was obviously angry with me for persuading Sandy to end the relationship with Dawn. She was displeased with this and blamed Jim for having been discovered in the wardrobe. As Sandy had refused to see Dawn again, she had instructed Jim to persuade Sandy to talk to her. But when he did, he still would not change his mind. The whole balance of forces between them had been upset by Sandy's withdrawal. It left Jim alone with Dawn, which neither of them wanted.

As we supported Sandy, Jim had to back off, and he left in a sulk. Sandy thanked us for our support, but wished to drop the matter, as it caused him considerable discomfort.

The next raid was destined to resolve the situation. It was a cool evening as we made our way over the Channel to our target. Soon we saw several other aircraft exploding. It seemed strange to us at first, until the same thing happened to us. There was an enormous explosion at the back of the plane and a cry from Jim in the rear turret. A German fighter, a Junkers, had attacked us from beneath. We went into a dive and only recovered after a few thousand feet. By some miracle, one of the other gunners had managed to hit the fighter, which went down. Once our craft was righted, it was obvious that we had sustained severe damage to the control surfaces, as the plane could hardly be controlled and was not responding well. There was a large hole in the floor just in front of the rear turret, while Jim was slightly hurt.

Sandy decided to jettison the bombs and attempt to return to base. He needed assistance with the controls; it took two of us to turn the stick. The engines were not damaged, only the back of the plane, so we stood a reasonable chance of returning.

Over the Channel again, we managed to get Jim out from his turret by assisting him round the enormous hole in the floor. But to his horror, his parachute was badly damaged, and we had no spare. At this point, we all became very worried indeed, for it seemed increasingly unlikely that we could land the plane, given the damage it had sustained. In fact, Sandy soon said that we would have to bale out. Jim gave him an intense, challenging look. Sandy just said that it had nothing to do with their quarrel. He explained that if they did not bale out soon, none of them would get out alive, as the plane was likely to go out of control at any minute.

One of the other gunners volunteered to take Jim with him in his 'chute. We managed to find some rope to tie the two men together. Just as we crossed the English coast, it was clear that we had to bale out as soon as possible. Jim and the other gunner baled out first, followed by the rest of us. Sandy was the last to go, once he had tried to take the plane as far as he could. In fact, this was not that far at all, and for a while we feared that the plane would land on him or us, as it quickly dropped from the sky. It was a sad moment when we saw a bright orange glow followed by a massive explosion, as the faithful old Lancaster was lost.

I had managed to survive the fall, though I was bruised all over. I narrowly missed a railway line. One of the others had their 'chute caught up in a moving train, but luckily managed to release it in time.

After a while, we regrouped. We had all survived except for Jim. Apparently, once the parachute had opened, the rope worked itself loose and the gunner could not keep hold of Jim.

We were all silent for some time. I felt a strange mixture of sadness and relief. I thought for a moment of asking the gunner if he had loosened the rope himself, but I thought better of it. I suspected we all had the same thought, but we did not want to know the truth.

Later, Jim was replaced by a friendly young man, who fitted in well, and we tried to forget what had happened to Jim.

Soon after Jim's death, Sandy approached Dawn again, in order to continue their relationship. I believe that he even asked her to marry him. However, she was not interested in him any more. She made it plain that she had wanted the two men, not one of them. The two had complimented one another; each had made up for the deficiencies in the other. Well, that was how she saw it, and he could not persuade her otherwise. She no longer found him attractive without his rival and partner. Though I suppose he could have foreseen her attitude, he was still devastated by it. Mind you, it sobered him up, so much so that he hardly touched alcohol for the rest of the war.

We were assigned to a new plane, became part of the elite corps of Bomber Command, and somehow survived, physically at least. But Sandy lost his boyish gaiety, and the gunner who was roped to Jim later suffered a severe depression. I have not seen the crew since the end of the war. I have always shunned the reunions. It was all too difficult.

Journal

In a sense, the last part of this painful story—the chilling bit when the rope became undone—summarised the situation: the three of them had been tied together in a desperate threesome and then, when Sandy wanted out, the threads unravelled. Indeed, the threads of my patient's life took some time to gather together after his wartime experiences. The constant bombing, wreaking havoc on those below, took its toll, particularly when the camaraderie was disturbed.

I could not bear the idea of outsiders being present in my relationship. Yet in a sense there are always other people present in a love relation, even if only in fantasy. There is that famous Freud quote that every sexual act is a process in which four people are involved. You could probably add a few more people for good measure. I suppose that some people need to have a real other looking on in order to make the sexual act feel real. It must be rather like having sex in front of a mirror. There you are at it, while there's someone looking on, and that in turn excites you. Double the bodies and double the excitement. Some people become so confused about their own body that they may need to see someone else observing to give them a sense of reality, while others just need the confusion.

The three in the story could not deal with being separate people. They fell into an arrangement that prevented them from feeling their own individuality. They lost themselves in the muddle, but they also found that exciting. They were turned on by muddle. At least, Jim and Dawn were; Sandy appeared to be a more reluctant participant, though his reluctance might have been part of the compulsive scenario.

Dawn was something of an enigma. Perhaps that was her fascination, particularly in the middle of that very masculine world, where women could easily become fantasy figures. It was not the sort of environment that encouraged ordinary relationships between the sexes. The threesome disturbed the equilibrium of the male fighting force, and interfered with their ruthless task of destruction. Again, there is the theme of a loss of balance, of a disturbance to an established equilibrium. It is clearly my current preoccupation.

I have been having sexual fantasies towards a younger colleague I met at a conference. Actually, she reminds me of the Dawn character, she also has a slightly wicked smile. She is a trainee and should be off-limits to more senior analysts like myself. She came up to me for advice, and I could not help noticing that she had no ring on her fingers. I do not usually look at fingers in this way. I do not mind indulging in sexual fantasies when I see or encounter an attractive woman. But I feel that at the moment I am in danger of enacting them.

Kathy is soon going on a three-day annual conference, leaving me (and the au pair) with the kids. Though I shall miss her as usual, I do not at these times feel too nervous about what she (and now I) might get up to. We have sometimes joked about having affairs, and have in the past been certain that, unlike some of our friends, we would not indulge ourselves.

How do I deal with my anger? It is one of the most difficult emotions to handle, especially in our culture. Kathy and I never really get angry with one another. Perhaps we should. It might be relief to have a flaming row. But there seems to be something in me that will not allow it. What did I say before about analysts being crippled?

I must keep control of myself. I can feel that I am beginning to fall apart. I am not attending adequately to my patients. I can barely follow what they say to me. I am becoming increasingly obsessed by my own thoughts, an occupational hazard.

I have decided not to approach that trainee. I am too dangerous at the moment. Perhaps I should stop making these jottings; they may be counter-productive because they are becoming too important to me. They are allowing me to create an enclosed and secret world. On the other hand, I feel an urge to write, as if my life depended on it. Perhaps that is a bit melodramatic. I must be wary of self-pity. After all, nothing may be seriously wrong.

I feel empty inside. I know there is something wrong. I have tried talking to Kathy, but we get nowhere. She tells me about the many stresses in her work. When I ask her if everything is all right between us she dismisses my concerns, but she does not reassure me. She makes me anxious, and I can see how my anxiety irritates her. She has begun to withdraw from me, which only increases my anxiety and in turn makes her withdraw further.

I am a great worrier. I must be difficult to live with, though there have been times when my worrying was quite useful. For example, when our daughter was born by an emergency caesarean. Kathy said that because I worried so much about what was happening, she was able to be more relaxed about it. It was indeed touch and go when she was born. Our daughter was in some distress, as was I, while Kathy was fairly light-headed on pethidine and the epidural. Finally, they decided to operate, and it turned out that the umbilical cord was round our daughter's neck. Luckily she turned out fine and was alert. But the whole experience brought me near to the possibility of death and disaster. Just a few more minutes and my daughter might have died or, worse, become a vegetable.

The feelings were so intense at that time. There was so much love between Kathy and me when the children were babies; it flowed everywhere. Where has it gone? Is it still there but hiding, or has it drained away?

Recently, our sexual activity has increased in frequency and intensity, as if we were struggling to survive. There is a desperation to our love-making, which is both exciting and worrying. Fiddling while Rome burns comes to mind. While making love, I sometimes have the image of the two of us struggling on a cliff top, just a few feet from the cliff's edge. We are holding onto one another for dear life, and yet our struggle may force us over the edge.

These thoughts seem to have pushed me to create a story about a couple I once saw for marital work, the result of which was not terribly successful. I have called the story "Repetitions", as it concerns how the past may repeat itself in the present, a common theme in psychoanalysis. History itself is a kind of fiction, a sort of story-writing. Once you look back at the past, you have already altered history, or have begun to create it in the looking back. In a sense, we are constantly creating or rewriting history.

Repetitions

The couple I saw could not, unfortunately, have their own children, and so decided to adopt. As I am concerned here with the effect of the past on the present, I shall go into the history of the couple in some detail before tackling their current relationship.

Paul was in his late thirties, an intelligent and quiet man, thoughtful and fairly sensitive. His mother died from cancer when he was nine. As a result, there was something missing in him, some terrible emptiness lingering in his heart. He coped well enough at the time of her death. Everyone commented that he was a brave little boy. Though missing his mother, Paul did not cry much. He expected her to return from hospital, as she had on many other occasions. It was difficult for him to believe she was gone forever. Did they mean a week? She had once gone for a week, and it had felt to him as if she had gone for ever. They had not let him see her body, just the coffin. So he still felt she might come back. She might be a different mum, but she would return.

After a few months, the forever seemed to get longer. By the time he realised that she would not return he had got sort of used to his sad father and he being alone together in their lonely house in north London, and he did not feel like crying much. He never really cried for her, not with his whole heart.

His father would often reminisce about Paul's mother, mostly recalling the good times and forgetting their many rows. She had been irritated by her husband's lack of ambition, and was always trying to push him to get on, without much success. The father hoped that Paul would fulfil his mother's ambitions and that, unlike him, would become a great success in life. Indeed, Paul did well at school and won a scholarship to Cambridge to study history. He was good at his studies and wrote some interesting essays. Like many young people, he also wrote poetry; the poems were brief but intense, with strong images. At Cambridge, he became part of a circle of rather serious young people who recited their poetry to one another and talked philosophy into the early hours.

He began his first serious relationship in his last year. Jessica was the daughter of one of his father's few friends. Paul met her when he came down to London for a weekend. She was married but going through a difficult divorce to a violent man. Jessica's parents had divorced when she was twelve, and her father then left the country. She never discovered what had gone wrong between them, as her mother was a tight-lipped woman who disliked displays of emotion, and her father made no direct contact with her. It was as if he had died.

Jessica's mother was comfortably off, thanks to an inheritance she received after the divorce. But she kept a tight rein on her money. She and Jessica led a frugal existence. Although the house was kept immaculately clean, there were few luxuries. New clothes were only bought on special occasions, once or twice a year. Holidays were spent at the same boarding house in Bournemouth.

Jessica was a well-behaved girl. Her only indulgence was food, which she devoured avidly. She was "large-boned" and plump, with a moon-shaped face, a small mouth, and a slight squint. The latter was inadequately corrected, so that she never quite looked at you straight in the eye. She was a good worker, both at home and at school. She liked being a good girl, but as a result was unpopular with other children. Rather than allow herself to be upset by this, she maintained a lofty, unaffected attitude. She was thus lonely at school, with few friends.

Puberty came as a profound shock to Jessica. Her body changes unfortunately coincided with the breakdown of her parents' marriage. She had had no hint that things were not right; family life had apparently continued smoothly, with no open quarrels or disagreements. Her parents appeared to be the best of friends, they were always polite to each other and to her. Her father, a bank manager, seemed the epitome of respectability and reliability. But soon after her twelfth birthday, he ran off with his secretary. Her mother simply could not believe that he could turn his back on the well-ordered life they had built up. She refused to talk to him or see him, except through her solicitor. Jessica missed her father very much, although in reality he had had little to do with her, because he worked long hours and left her care to her mother.

As her adolescence advanced, Jessica began to show one or two signs of rebellion. She began to question her mother's controlling attitude. She refused to keep her room spotlessly clean, although by normal standards it was still tidy. She demanded better and more interesting clothes, and she began to take an interest in boys, albeit at first from a cautious distance.

When she went to a university outside London, she felt free for the first time in her life. She plunged into student society, then fell head over heels in love with her first boyfriend, a fellow student in his final year, the first man to pay her serious attention. They met at the college music club and enjoyed going to concerts together. Gerald, a tall, lean man, the opposite in build of her father, who was small and rotund, was polite and courteous to her. She found it easy talking to him and he seemed a ready listener.

As their relationship developed, she began to notice that he drank rather a lot, which made him irascible and occasionally verbally aggressive, which, strangely, drew her closer to him. He was an adopted child, and felt, rightly or wrongly, that his adoptive parents never really accepted him, particularly after his mother conceived her own child soon after he was brought home. Jessica felt sorry for him. She had also had a lonely childhood and could understand his insecurity. For all his faults, Gerald gave her more physical affection than she had received from her parents, and she hoped that in time she could help him with his drinking.

They married, despite, or perhaps because of, the disapproval of her mother, who had higher expectations for her. For a while she enjoyed life. She was a good home-maker, and she made their tiny flat comfortable and cosy. Gerald seemed to appreciate her efforts to make their life pleasant and smooth. However, it was not long before he found his stability stifling. He became hostile and aggressive to her for no good reason. He made fun of her efforts to please him and he found fault with everything she did, and also with her appearance. Because she had such a poor self-image, she did little to defend herself against these attacks.

At night he spent hours away from home and returned drunk and aggressive. However, there were times when he sobered up and was tender and sweet to her, which gave her the hope and courage to stick it out with him.

On the day she received her degree, he beat her up badly, and she finally left him. She sought refuge, however reluctantly, in her mother's house. It was there, one weekend, that she met Paul. She liked him very much from the start. He was quiet and thoughtful, such a pleasant contrast to her husband. Paul found talking to her easy and comforting. He could feel protective towards her, as she had had such a bad time with her husband and was obviously a vulnerable and needy person. Gerald had exploited her vulnerability, but Paul felt that he could protect her. He was also needy himself, but shy of too much contact. Jessica offered him just enough love to make him feel wanted but not so much that he would retreat into his protective shell.

Gerald tried to contact her several times, but her mother refused to let him speak to her. He wrote letters threatening to come round and take her back, but he never carried out his threats and soon the letters and the calls ceased.

It was not long before Jessica spent weekends at Cambridge with Paul. She rather took over his life. Instead of studying, he spent much of his free time with her. She became reliant on his quiet strength; he felt stronger in her presence. The result was that he obtained a disappointing lower second and gave up any hope of an academic career. Instead, he became a secondary school teacher, a job he did well and learned to enjoy.

They were married as soon as her divorce came through. Her mother was at last content with Jessica's choice, for although Paul was unlikely to become wealthy, at least he was steady and was one of "their set." Paul's father was particularly pleased with his choice, but at the same time also sad to be left at home on his own.

Their married life was orderly and content. Paul had at last found the domestic peace and routine for which he had undoubtedly craved since his mother's death, while Jessica had found a man willing to accept her desire for order and respectability. She no longer felt at all rebellious towards her mother. They even got along well on occasions.

There was, however, one painful gap in their otherwise contented life—no children arrived. This was a terrible blow for Jessica, who was desperate to look after a dependent little being, particularly after her bad experiences with her first husband, who had left her feeling bad about herself and her body. She felt that she was made for motherhood. Her job, in a publishing house, did not make up for the gap in her life. Paul was less bothered by their infertility, for he had enough interests to keep himself busy, and his career was progressing well.

As time passed, Jessica became increasingly desperate for children. Her dreams were full of pregnant women, nursing mothers, and her own fantasy children. She could hardly bear to look at pregnant women in the street, and she would avoid them where possible. Finally, she persuaded Paul to go with her for an investigation of their problem. This proved to be particularly upsetting for her when he was found to be normal and her uterus abnormal. They attempted various artificial means of conception without success, until they eventually accepted that adoption was their only chance of having a family. They then had to go through an extended and, to them, humiliating process of vetting before being accepted as potential parents. The social worker they saw had doubts about their parenting capacities since she detected in Paul an absence of positive feeling towards the prospect of having children. But Jessica's more definite wish for them carried the day.

They waited some three years before they were suddenly informed that a baby was waiting to be collected. His natural mother, a student, had been unable to look after him. It felt very strange driving to the agency with a carry-cot to pick up a child as if it were an item of shopping. They took the little bundle home and began caring for it. The baby was a contented little boy, about three weeks old. He took what he was offered without much fuss. Jessica took to the baby fairly easily and performed all her motherly duties with care and concern.

They were very surprised that little Jonathan slept right through the first night, for they expected to be woken up at least once. They sat downstairs watching television, listening anxiously to the baby alarm, expecting and even hoping that the baby would wake and cry for them. On a number of occasions throughout the night, they went upstairs to check that he was still breathing.

Because he was so little trouble, they feared that something was dreadfully wrong with him, and they even had the unrealistic thought of returning him in the morning in exchange for another baby. But they soon dismissed such thoughts as the result of panic and inexperience.

In due course, they became used to Jonathan's ways and he to theirs, and life was relatively calm and peaceful. His development proceeded normally, and he became a friendly toddler, very close to his mother. Paul was fond of "the boy," as he called him, but was not intimately involved with him in the first few months. He became more interested in him when he was able to play with bricks. Paul discouraged him from knocking them down, so that from an early age Jonathan became an unusual child, in that he rarely made a mess.

After a couple of years, they applied to take another child. Sophie's first night with them, at four weeks old, was very different from that of Jonathan. She bawled her tiny eyes out, and it was hours before she finally cried herself to sleep. She was a demanding baby, hungry for milk and constantly crying for attention. Jessica was exhausted by her demands and resented being woken up at least twice a night for several months. Jonathan was jealous of his baby sister at first, and began to demand attention from both parents, which only added to the stress.

After many months, Sophie settled at night, though she remained what they considered a "difficult" child. She would not be satisfied by the rather minimal physical contact offered by Jessica and Paul. She was desperate for cuddles and would cling to her mother when she was about to be put in her bed.

Jessica and Paul decided to tell their children early on that they were adopted. By the time that they had both started school, the children were left in no doubt that mummy and daddy had picked them up from the adoption agency and that, while of course they were very much wanted, it was also made clear that they came from somewhere else, a place which felt cold and uninviting to both children.

Displays of negative emotion, particularly anger, were discouraged. For example, if the children felt anger coming on, they had to go to the shed at the bottom of the garden in order to scream. The children began to be frightened of their mother's disapproval, because as they became older, she became more strict with them. Their lives were regulated by rules and by the need to be good. Bad behaviour was unacceptable and was immediately dealt with by punishments such as being sent to the bedroom without a meal, or by the withholding of some reward.

Paul was not a natural disciplinarian, but he went along with his wife's attitude. But, in addition, he began to display barely disguised disdain for her. His conversation and tone of voice was invariably spiced with implied criticism and condescension. Yet he was unconscious of his hatred. He could not be openly angry with her, although he was with the children. She was fleetingly aware that he despised her and resented her inability to have children, but she generally considered that they were a happy couple and devoted parents. In a sense, they were indeed devoted to the children, but with an attitude of professional workers rather than ordinary parents. Genuine and open love was missing, except between the children themselves. They played together for hours and were affectionate with one another.

In time, they sharply allied themselves against their parents, and a great divide was created between adult and child worlds. The children reluctantly followed adult rules, while spontaneity, messiness, and childishness were kept upstairs in the childrens' bedrooms, where they created a harsh imaginary world of fat demons and monsters, which were destroyed by fantasy heroes.

Jonathan was a disappointment to his father, as he showed little sign of having any interest in academic studies. Sophie, who was brighter, was perceived by her parents as essentially naughty and rebellious, a constant torment to them.

While family life was tolerable when the children were young, their adolescence brought with it major problems, because the children attempted to throw off their parents' straitjacket of rules, expectations, and misperceptions.

Jessica was at a loss as to how to control them. Paul seemed unaware of his own contribution to the difficulties, blaming the children for their own bad behaviour. Of course, by the time that they were adolescent, they had begun to have confirmed personalities. Sophie was wilful. She would not tidy her room, and insisted on wearing way-out clothes and masses of make-up. Jonathan's rebellion was quieter, although no less determined. He told lies to his father about how he was studying. Since he could not hide his poor grades, there were frequent rows about his lack of effort.

Sophie was interested in boys from an early age. She was attractive, with a lively face, a mop of ginger hair and a trim figure. Jonathan was more socially inhibited, though good-looking, tall, and lean, with a pleasant, self-deprecating smile. She liked to talk to him about her sexual feelings. These conversations were a natural continuation of their childhood intimacy. There was the added excitement in the awareness that their parents would be deeply shocked if they were to listen in.

The children also shared a deep and unsettling feeling about their origins. The knowledge that they were unrelated by blood, either with one another or with their parents, increased the excitement of their intimate talks. They were curious about their natural parents. They were told that both their mothers were educated and young but unable to provide a suitable home for them. This explanation, though accurate as far as it went, was accompanied by an added implication that their natural mothers had misbehaved, and that Jonathan and Sophie were incredibly lucky to have been rescued from a life of poverty and shame.

Far from making them grateful to their parents, this attitude made them create a romantic past for themselves, in which both their natural mothers were victims of society's harsh and uncaring attitudes. They also felt that their mothers had let their sexual impulses rule them, a notion which they found liberating and exciting—and so different from the controlling and insipid attitude of their parents.

Jessica and Paul shared little of their own past lives with the children, perhaps because they feared having to tackle the issue of the natural parents. If they had, it might have given the children a greater sense of their own identity and an affinity with their parents, as well as reducing the mystery of their origins.

Paul became more and more of a recluse, apparently indifferent to his family. He hid in his study, where he pored over books and occupied himself with his career as headmaster of a large secondary school, where he was a respected figure of authority.

Jonathan's interest in sex was aroused by his sister. They began to explore each other's bodies with curiosity and awe. What began as a game soon turned into a full sexual relationship when Sophie was fifteen and Jonathan nearly seventeen. Although initiated by Sophie, Jonathan became more eager to continue the relationship than she was. He became obsessed by her. She tried to cool the relationship by appealing to their sense of guilt, to no avail. He was driven by his passion for her. They had shared so much together as children that to him their sexual relationship seemed a natural continuation of their childhood fantasy games. Furthermore, there was no blood tie to contaminate it. It provided the warmth and closeness that they both desired and did not receive from their parents.

At first, they took care not to be discovered but, as time went on, they took greater and greater risks. They even had sex in the early evening, while supposedly getting on with their homework.

Sophie continued to see other boys, with whom she had various sexual encounters, but Jonathan remained faithful to her. She did not keep her activities secret from him, even though it provoked jealous scenes. Indeed, she hoped that she might provoke him to leave her alone, but without success.

They became even more isolated from their parents. Paul became indifferent to them and left the parenting to Jessica, who was at a loss as what to do for the best.

The situation came to a head when Sophie became pregnant by Jonathan. He was stunned when she told him; it had never occurred to him that he might become a father, even though they had not been strict about contraception. Sophie was matter-of-fact about the situation. She had been vaguely aware of dicing with fate. The risk of conceiving a child had given her added excitement. Furthermore, it gave her an enormous advantage over her mother. She could relish the sense of triumph over her. Having a baby would make her a real woman, unlike her mother. And there was in the background the almost conscious wish to be like her natural mother, who had become pregnant when young and single.

She finally decided to tell her mother one evening, in the kitchen. "Look, mum," she began tentatively, "I have something important to tell you."

"Well, go on then, if you must," Jessica replied, sorting out washing for the tumble dryer.

"Well, you see, I am not feeling that well."

"Yes, I noticed you've looked a bit peaky recently. You don't eat properly. I keep telling you."

"It's not that." Sophie hesitated for a while. She wanted to run somewhere. Anywhere else would have felt warmer and safer. But the thought of the baby inside her focused her thoughts.

"I haven't got all day, dear," said Jessica, either ignoring or not noticing her daughter's distress.

"I am pregnant!" said Sophie at last.

There was a long silence. Jessica seemed not to have heard. She carried on loading the tumble dryer as if nothing had happened, and refused to look directly at Sophie. Sophie was about to give up on her mother and leave the room, when Jessica shouted at her viciously: "Don't you leave this room!"

"Please don't start on me, mum. I can't deal with it," Sophie pleaded, with tears welling up.

"How could you!" said Jessica with emotion.

"I don't know. I just did."

"You're only fifteen. It's ridiculous."

"I knew you wouldn't understand. I'm wasting my time."

"Who's the father?" Jessica demanded.

"Well, that's the point," said Sophie, screwing up her face and nervously running her hands through her mop of ginger hair.

"You mean, you don't even know?" said Jessica with distaste.

"Oh, I know all right. I think you'd better sit down."

"Don't play with me, my girl. Just tell me the truth and don't waste my time."

"Oh, for Christ's sake, if that's your bloody attitude," she retorted. "You're impossible. Look, it's Jonathan. He's the bloody father!"

Jessica was stunned by this further revelation. She turned her blanched face to Sophie and for first time looked straight at her. "You don't know what you're saying," she said, in a whisper.

"Jo and I have been having sex," said Sophie defiantly. "Sex!"

"Where is Jonathan?" said Jessica, distraught.

"He's upstairs. He doesn't want to come down now."

"It's not true, is it?" asked Jessica suspiciously, thinking that this must be another of Sophie's wind-ups. "You're just saying this to shock me."

"Not this time, mum." Sophie lifted up her T-shirt to reveal the slight swelling in her abdomen. "Feel it, mum," she added with a triumphant smile.

Jessica turned away and mumbled half to herself, "What will your father say?"

"Who cares?" Sophie said with disdain.

"You stupid child!" Jessica screamed with anger, and hit Sophie hard across the cheek, making her cry with pain.

"You bitch!" Sophie shouted, holding her cheek.

"Don't you see?" said Jessica. "Don't you see what you've done?"

Sophie began to sob, and then Jessica suddenly felt guilty about hitting her. She approached her as if to comfort her, but Sophie drew away.

"Go away, you stupid fat cow. You're not my fucking mother. You've never wanted to be," she cried tearfully.

"That's not fair. You're my daughter. I love you."

"Bullshit."

Jessica managed to calm down, and took a grip of herself. "Look, Sophie, now it's your turn to hear the truth."

"What do you mean?" said Sophie, through her tears.

"I shouldn't tell you on your own. Your father made me promise to keep it a secret, but I can't now."

"What is it, for Christ's sake?" asked Sophie insistently, no longer crying. "Tell me. I have a right to know."

"Well, it's about Jo's parents. We were told. We were warned about it. But if we hadn't agreed to accept him, we might have to have waited more years for another baby. You see, his parents were brother and sister."

Sophie did not know whether to laugh or cry. She held onto her stomach and once more burst into tears, repeating over, "I want my baby. Don't take my baby."

Needless to say, their lives were transformed by Sophie's and Jessica's revelations. Jonathan became depressed and kept to his room. Paul was devastated by the news, and then became very angry with the others. Instead of offering help to them, he opted out of any responsibility. He felt that what had happened was the final straw, the end of a long succession of humiliations caused by Jessica and the children. He felt that his married life had been an illusion, and very soon he left home.

Jessica, however, came into her own. For the first time, she felt close to her daughter, and offered her help and support. Sophie eventually had the baby, though she managed to keep its paternity a secret. Jonathan came out of his depression, but remained a vulnerable young man. He improved somewhat when he left home to train as a teacher, for once following in Paul's footsteps.

The baby became a source of great pleasure for Jessica as well as Sophie. Jessica took on most of the day-to care so that Sophie could continue her education. Jessica at last felt fulfilled as a woman. She was sad that Paul had left, but had few regrets about the stand she had taken. She even stood up to her mother's disapproving comments. Jessica was determined that Sophie's baby would not be given away. Sophie calmed down, and became less driven by anger and grievance.

Journal

There are so many threads to this story that I am not sure where to begin my commentary. Of course, infertility is a terrible curse. Fear of it has become a major anxiety as, these days, professional women often decide to try for children well into their thirties. When Kathy and I had the children, we were just over thirty and the oldest in the ante-natal class, whereas now we would be among the younger ones.

Paul and Jessica's inability to have children left them with a terrible emptiness at the heart of their marriage, which they tried to fill with their adopted children. But Sophie and Jonathan never came up to expectations, nor could they ever do so as long as their parents had not sorted out their own relationship.

Psychoanalysts often have to deal with incestuous fantasies from patients, but even so it is never easy to take in the full impact of actual incest, however understandable the context in which it has taken place. Clearly, part of the reason that the children turned to each other was the absence of parental warmth. The additional factor driving the drama was the power of the past, from a variety of sources. There was the lack of mothering in Paul's early life. Jessica became a sort of mother to him, but he could not forgive her for not being able to bear him children. Thus she remained a kind of fantasy mother, and his own earlier maternal loss was repeated with his wife, making him withdraw into himself.

The children were driven to commit incest by powerful forces beyond their control and conscious awareness. There were combined forces from their natural and adoptive parents' pasts, illustrating the power of repetition, of how the past can be repeated over and over in the present. This is perhaps particularly the case when the past is not given due respect—neither Jessica nor Paul wished to share much of their own past with the children, nor did they allow the children to know about their natural parents, until Jessica was forced by circumstances to reveal the truth.

There seemed to be little evidence of strong incestuous feelings between the parents and the children. Indeed, there was not enough emotional contact between them. A few incestuous feelings may have done them some good.

The story highlights how trauma can be transmitted from one generation to another, in modified and in direct forms. There were various traumas in the family—Paul's loss of his mother, Jessica's loss of her father, and the incest in Jonathan's past. Relevant in this context was that the incest in the present took place in the absence of genuine fatherly authority in the family. Paul was an ineffectual father, unable to stand up to his adolescent children. He just opted out of his responsibilities when the going got tough, so that there was no father to provide safe boundaries within the family.

The parents also had difficulty in showing genuine feeling. The hatred between them could not be openly acknowledged, so that it was never dealt with or modified. Perhaps if it had been, then the children might not have been driven to repeat the cycle of trauma. However, at least Jessica managed to rally to her daughter's aid, thus hopefully putting an end to the cycle of repetition of destructive family relationships.

Was this story a warning for me to face the terrible truth of my own family situation? Why on earth did I become an analyst and find myself caught up in people's suffering? What about my own suffering? I do know that my mother was somewhat depressed after I was born. I am certain that has something to do with my becoming an analyst, which involves trying to sort out other people's minds. Maybe that is also why I find it difficult coping with Kathy's stress. I have been so accustomed to her being strong and capable that I am made anxious by her being vulnerable and depressed ...

I have never been a romantic bloke, not the kind to bring home flowers and such like. But I have begun to feel romantic towards Kathy. I want to spoil her, take her out for a treat, indulge her. But I am afraid that she will think me foolish and will reject my offers. The uncertainty about our relationship has begun to stir up all sorts of new notions about myself. Middle age is, of course, supposed to be a time to reconsider your life, or at least an opportunity to take stock of what has been in order to cope with what is to come.

I wonder if I am a repressed romantic, dying to have some woman whom I can worship. Kathy has never struck me as being the type of woman who wanted such adulation. She is very logical, clear-thinking and down to earth. I have relied on her clear-sightedness about ordinary life and her social skills. But perhaps we need to shift our attitudes to one another. I recall that her father was a romantic at heart, and that they had a very close relationship. I suppose that I was his polar opposite, and that was partly why she fell for me; she had had enough exposure at home to the romantic male. But, then, I have allowed something important in myself to be suppressed. Should I consider changing? And for what reason? Would something essential be lost if I were to change, or does all change feel like some kind of loss?

I am having troubled dreams about death, though I am fit and well in myself. Perhaps I sense a kind of death looming, that of my marriage. The prospect of our relationship ending is unbearable. We have built up a life together, created a home and brought up children. Until now, we have faced and mastered countless daily anxieties. Separation would be like a death. Yet she has become more separate from me. I have begun to talk to her about my anxieties, but she still feels increasingly unreachable. My stories are attempts to reach out somewhere, now that she is not really there for me. Perhaps in the past I relied on her too much. I have been like a parasite, living off her while not being myself, whatever that is. This time could be an opportunity to reshape both our lives. Yet being solitary after so much time as two entwined beings is difficult. Being one is a different kind of mathematics from being two. Being one while also being two is very advanced maths indeed.

These stories are producing messages from somewhere. They have a life of their own. I have begun to think that they almost come from another person. Once a story is finished, I just want to move on. Then when I re-read what I have written, I do not feel like their author. Yet they arise from the most intimate part of myself. I take notes for them between seeing patients, at any spare moment, just before going to sleep, and sometimes in the middle of the night. I work up my notes into a draft, and then type out the final story. I am becoming attached to the process of writing. It is taking me over. When Kathy returns home, she talks to me at length about her work but I only pretend to listen to her now. I am really trying to figure out the next move in one of my stories. Her real-life stories leave me cold. I have heard about her many stresses and strains at work so many times that I now switch off. I try to hide my eyes from her, for if she could see into them, she would know that I am somewhere else. I am somewhere else in order to be more myself. Fine words. The fact is, I am in anxious hiding, while my shadow continues to have conversations around the dinner table. Hence, perhaps, the title of my next story, based on another patient, The Shadow of Death. A gloomy-sounding title but, in this case, death becomes a source of attraction to the living, even a kind of marriage broker. I treated the patient some time ago, and followed him up after treatment ended. I have, as always, distorted the facts, both for the sake of the story and also to protect the patient's identity.

The shadow of death

It began with a funeral, which was not exactly an auspicious place to start an affair; you would have thought it more suitable for the ending of a relationship.

I shall call my main character Simon Shadow, for reasons that will soon become apparent. He had come to pay his last respects to his late partner, Jim Sinclair, who had died suddenly from a massive heart attack at the tragically early age of forty-four, leaving behind a widow, Jane, and three young children. Sinclair had smoked, eaten, drunk, and worked to excess. In the early days of their law firm, they had put in an enormous amount of time and effort to set it on its feet. But even when the firm was doing well, Sinclair worked and worried excessively.

Shadow was in his late thirties and unmarried. Though he had come close to marriage on several occasions, he had managed to avoid the final commitment. He would live with a woman for several months but towards the end of the eighth month or so, just as things were moving to a satisfactory climax, he would insist on breaking up the relationship. He would look at other women, refuse to make love, or make love with indifference. He might pretend he was seeing another woman, or just admit that he had no intention of marrying and that he was a pig. On the occasion of the funeral, he was free and on the look-out for another woman.

Shadow's mother had died soon after his birth, but he never discovered the cause of her death; it remained shrouded in mystery and confusion. Perhaps that had something to do with his relationship difficulties. He obtained little information from his father about her, except that she had had some kind of illness. But he was no wiser concerning the nature of the illness. Vague thoughts that she might have killed herself or was murdered occasionally occurred to him. You could say that he lived subsequently in the shadow of his mother's unexplained death, and that his personality never quite developed to the full, that he was a shadow of what he could have become. Hence the name.

Perhaps it was no surprise, given his history, that Shadow was obsessed with crime from an early age and became addicted to detective stories. His interest in death and murder had also no doubt helped to shape his choice of profession. He specialised in criminal law, relying on his late partner to attend to civil cases as well as the firm's administration. His loss was a great personal as well as a professional blow. They had been great chums; they were able to share professional and private concerns, and offered one another considerable mutual support. Shadow also looked up to Sinclair as a successful family man, and greatly enjoyed spending time at his house. Shadow got on well with the children, and was accepted as an honorary member of the family, even spending Christmas lunches with them.

The funeral was well attended, with many friends and family members crowding into the crematorium for the service. One of the women attracted Shadow's attention. She was Sinclair's sister-in-law, an attractive women in her mid-thirties, with a rather pale complexion. Her face reminded him of some marble sculpture. She was standing next to her sister, with an eye on the children and one arm supporting Sinclair's frail, elderly mother. She seemed to exude strength and support.

He vaguely recalled that he had seen her before at Sinclair's house. Her name was Margaret. She had made little impression on him before. What was it, then, he wondered, that had so stirred him? He was full of grief over his friend's death. The occasion was terribly sad, many people cried openly, and the three little children looked lost and perplexed. It seemed positively indecent to feel sexual attraction in such an atmosphere.

The service was brief but moving. It included some of his partner's favourite jazz pieces and a tribute spoken through tears by an old friend. The worst moment was when the coffin began to be wheeled into the furnace. It seemed to travel painfully slowly, as if reluctant to go, pulled back by the yearning thoughts of the living. The machinery also produced an irritating squeak every few seconds, which sullied the occasion.

When at last the doors of the furnace opened and the coffin disappeared, the widow could no longer keep control. She produced an agonising wail and collapsed into her sister's strong arms. Shadow rushed over to help, much to Margaret's relief. Their hands touched briefly as they each put an arm round Jane to support her. She soon came round and burst into tears. Meanwhile, one of the crematorium staff motioned people to leave—another funeral party was waiting to use the hall.

Shadow and Margaret led the now crying children and their mother into the gardens, where they were to wait for the ashes. The other mourners filed out slowly, mainly in silence. Some spent some time examining the various wreathes laid out on the lawn. Eventually, Jane calmed down, let Margaret go and held the children to her in a sorrowful but comforting huddle. Margaret then spoke to Shadow: "Thank you. You're Jim's partner, aren't you?"

"That's right," he replied softly.

"Terrible shock for everyone. Mind you, he didn't look after himself. Jane was always worried that something like this would happen. But it was all so sudden. The poor children."

"If there's anything I can do," he offered tentatively.

"I'll tell her. Presumably, he left them well provided for."

"Oh, yes. I drew up the will."

"Of course."

They were silent for a while, occasionally glancing at one another with curiosity and then looking away at the others.

"Are you coming back to the house?" she asked.

"Yes."

"Good."

There was another pause, then she said: "I'd better go now."

"Yes."

One of the staff had indicated that the ashes were ready. She went to collect them with her sister. Shadow decided to make his way back to the house. As he drove away, he was assailed by disturbing thoughts. He had an overwhelming desire to see Margaret again. He had never before had such powerful feelings for a woman. He tended to remain rather aloof towards them, being more interested in possessing their bodies than in having an intimate relationship. By nature he was physically undemonstrative, and yet he had a strong desire to touch Margaret and to be touched by her. He recalled with pleasure the brief moment when their hands had met round Jane's crumpled body. He felt suddenly vulnerable, and noticed inside himself a terrible fear that he might lose Margaret, even though they had only just met. He even became fearful lest she have an accident on the way back to the house.

Of course he felt sad about his partner's death, he had lost a friend and close associate who had given him much support over the years, through all his various amorous tangles and legal dilemmas. So he felt a certain amount of guilt and shame about having strong yearnings for Margaret on such a solemn day and in sight of the suffering of Jane and her children.

Despite these misgivings, he felt convinced that his feelings for Margaret were genuine. She had touched some deep chord within him, and he was determined to pursue her when the right moment should present itself.

Margaret was to stay with her sister for a few days to give her support. Shadow visited the family daily and soon became intimate with Margaret. She was a rich woman, thanks to the legacy from her late husband, a much older man, who had died of a stroke two years previously. There were no children—neither had been keen on them.

Margaret was a strong character, determined and decisive. She took charge of the family, organising the everyday activities for which Jane had little heart. Night time was particularly difficult for the children as they could not sleep easily, and insisted on spending the night in their mother's bedroom. Even then, they needed plenty of cuddles and stories from their aunt before finally nodding off.

Shadow came for tea and supper on a couple of occasions and helped with the children as best he could. Though it was very painful to be at such close quarters to extreme grief, he found it bearable and even compelling. Being close to death made him feel alive.

He was soon convinced that Margaret was the woman for him. His other relationships had begun with an early sexual seduction, but with her he felt cautious. Her desired her very much indeed, but he made no move to entice her into bed. Indeed, for some time he felt quite small and helpless in her presence.

About a week after the funeral, he had a vivid dream which pre-occupied him for some time. This struck him as odd, as he did not usually recall his dreams.

There was a dark female figure standing some distance from him. At first, he could not make out her features. After a while, her face became visible. It was dead white, like stone. She turned her gaze on him. He felt afraid but approached her. As he was about to touch her face, she became a statue, which then crumbled, as if it were made of fragile plaster.

He woke up in an agitated state. The statue at once reminded him of Margaret. At first, he feared that she might have died in the night. As he came to, he then felt strongly that the dream must be telling him to do something effective about Margaret before she returned to her home outside London, or else he would lose her, and all his hopes would crumble.

At last he plucked up courage to invite her out for a meal. She was happy to accept the invitation. They found themselves at a corner table in a good Chinese restaurant. It was only when they sat down and glanced through the menu that it occurred to them that they were at last alone. There were no children, no sad widow, and no arrangements to keep them occupied or distracted. It was an anxious moment. They were suddenly aware of one another, as if meeting for the first time. But it was not long before they once more felt at ease. He confessed that he had wanted to take her out for some time, but had not wanted to disrupt the family.

"That was very thoughtful of you," she said. "But I'm glad you finally asked."

"How are things now?"

"Oh, not so acute. I can leave soon. Then it'll be up to Jane to manage. It'll take a long time for them to get over this, if ever. Traumas don't just go away. They remain part of your landscape, parts of which come more or less into focus, depending on what is going on in your life."

"Well, you've been indispensable."

"I've done what I could. It's little enough, really."

They had ordered the food, and were awaiting the starters, when, to his surprise, he caught himself saying: "You look radiant."

She was somewhat taken aback. "Oh, er, thank you."

"I mean, you are amazing. Through all this trouble, you manage to look beautiful."

"I don't know what to say," she replied awkwardly.

"I've embarrassed you. I'm sorry."

"You've just taken me by surprise. I do like being with you."

"We get on."

"Yes. I didn't think ..."

"It was more than that," he said, finishing her sentence nervously.

"Well, not really."

"When I saw you at the funeral ..." He stopped himself lest he frighten her.

The food was then brought to them, so he stopped talking until the waiter had left. Then, as she tucked into a spare rib, she said gently: "Go on, I want to hear."

"You see," he began faultingly, and picking up some spicy prawns, "I have something to confess. I've never told anyone before. Oh, it sounds crazy."

"I do understand," she said, putting her small, delicate hand on his. He took hold of the hand and briefly stroked it gently.

"I don't know exactly how to put it," he said. "It was all that emotion. Something happened to me. I'm ashamed to tell you. But, anyway, you want to know. I felt alive, perhaps for the first time in my life. I haven't been the same since. You probably didn't notice anything. Forgive me. I'm talking too much. You must think me ridiculous. Like a child."

"Don't be silly," she said, giving his hand an affectionate squeeze. "I like what you say."

"Well, the fact is," he explained, "I have always been fascinated by the rituals of death. Do you think that's strange?"

"Haven't you noticed that I always wear black?" she replied.

"I thought it was because of the funeral."

"I never wear any other colour. Perhaps you think I'm strange."

"You're like me, then?"

"Yes. I'm drawn to death. It brings me out. The best thing my husband did for me was to die. That sounds terrible. He wasn't a bad man. I should be grateful to him, for he left me a lot of money. That's not what I'm referring to. There was no love between us. Some affection, though. He was a workaholic. The only peace he found was on his death bed. His face looked calm for the first time."

"You've no children? You're so good with them."

"He didn't want any. And I wasn't ready. Also, I am convinced that if I had a child, something terrible would happen to me or to it."

"My mother died just after I was born," he said with no emotion.

"How terrible. Who brought you up?"

"My father and then stepmother."

"You weren't happy?"

"Probably not," he replied dryly, not wishing to pursue that topic.

"My mother left home when I was ten. She had some sort of crisis. She regretted it, but my father wouldn't have her back. She remained depressed for the rest of her life. In permanent mourning."

"And are you?"

"I suppose I'm still waiting for the great loss of my life," she said with a laugh.

"You've never been in love?"

"Oh, I've had many infatuations. I've enjoyed them. But I've only ever given part of myself."

"Me, too. Maybe it's safer."

"I've had enough of safety," she said resolutely. "I married out of loneliness and boredom, or because I was tired of saying no. It was pleasant enough, but we lived separate lives. I wasted seven years. Not again."

They soon began seeing each other regularly. They stayed in one another's homes on alternate weekends, and maintained telephone contact during the week. Shadow was obsessed by her. Time away from her was torture. Yet he did not dare admit to her the depth of his feelings, in case she despised him. She was the first woman whom he had held in awe. The others had been much younger than him and rather insecure and needy. Margaret, however, was self-contained and mysterious.

He neglected his practice because she dominated his thoughts. Without his partner, the firm became an administrative mess.

Clients began to go elsewhere. Eventually, he was forced to find a new partner, which helped the business, but he remained in crisis. His world had been turned upside down. Before Margaret, he had put his career above everything else. But now, his love for her took over his life. He kept imagining he saw her in the street; he had imaginary conversations with her in the car; he pictured her beside him during lunch breaks. He rang her every day, sometimes several times a day, in order to keep in touch. She did not object to the calls—on the contrary, she encouraged them.

When they met, his desperation vanished, and he felt contented and secure. Only parting was difficult. They would hold onto one another for minutes on end, kissing and hugging, trying to separate but clinging to one another for fear of drowning in a sea of despair.

The time came when they had to consider the future. The week-end meetings were delightful but frustrating. Just as they felt comfortable with each other, it was time to part and to repeat the agonies of separation. Yet they were also afraid of deepening the relationship. He felt dependent on her; she was the focus for much of his day. She enjoyed his company, but was not obsessed with him. The constant separations were for her a particular source of excitement. They were like mini-deaths, rehearsals for the final and inevitable parting.

Nonetheless, they decided to marry. His enthusiasm for living together finally persuaded her to agree to marriage, even though she felt it was risky to change an arrangement that had given them both satisfaction and exquisite pain.

Initially, all seemed to go well. Their living arrangements remained the same for some time, as she did not wish to live in London, and he could not deal with his practice and commute daily from the country. But his own work continued to deteriorate, and he eventually sold his share. Once he had also sold his flat, he moved in with Margaret, in her large country house.

Though he had once been devoted to his profession, he no longer missed practising criminal law. Being with Margaret day and night was much more attractive to him. However, it was not long before she became irritated by his constant presence and yearned for a return to the old arrangement. Indeed, she even proposed buying him another flat in London, so he could leave her from time to time. He was bewildered by her suggestion, for he could no longer

imagine a day without seeing her. The only way she was able to create some space for herself was to keep her separate bedroom. At
least then there was the constant uncertainty about whether or not
they would come together for the night—she still craved the excitement of continually finding and losing him. But the sleeping
arrangements had an adverse effect on Shadow, who began to feel
anxious and neglected, which made him even more demanding and
irritating. For example, when she went to her bedroom for the night,
instead of leaving her alone he would knock on the door and plead
with her to spend the night with him. But, to his annoyance, she
would refuse to communicate with him at these times. By the morning, he would be in a dark mood, sulky and withdrawn. He would
eventually recover his spirits as the day wore on but, in the meantime, she would be so annoyed by his sulkiness that she would take
herself off to some distant part of the house and would refuse to
have anything to do with him.

There were occasional light-hearted moments, when they
would go out for a meal or have friends round. But when they were
alone, their relationship became tense and claustrophobic. They
continued to make love, but with an increasing sense of desperation, as if they were trying to patch up a fatal wound. At times, it
was more like making hate than love, for she would turn her body
away from him in order to be entered from behind—more from
unwillingness to look at his face than for a wish for pleasure. He
would thrust into her with aggressive strokes, each one more violent than the last, until he came into her, in his own time and with
little consideration for her.

The turning point in their relationship came a couple of weeks
after he had a bout of influenza. His left foot began to feel strange,
as if it did not belong to him. He thought no more of it until the
whole of his leg began to drag. In a short time, he was very ill
indeed. He had trouble moving all his limbs, and struggled for
breath. She took him to the local casualty department, where he collapsed, unable to breathe at all. He was rushed to the intensive care
unit and put on an artificial ventilator.

For days he was completely paralysed, and was kept traquil-
lised while hovering between life and death. Margaret stayed by his
bed through the day and much of the night, holding his floppy
hand, or helping to turn him. As he lay helpless, with tubes running

in and out of his ailing body, and with wires linking him to a heart monitor, she felt once more love and tenderness for him. He was helpless and, yes, she had to admit, so death-like. A living corpse. Her life had new meaning. She decided to devote all her energy to caring for him.

After a couple of weeks, he was more rousable and could sit with support. He could not speak as he was too weak, and also had to breathe through a tracheotomy, but he was able to mouth words, which she could understand. It was, of course, a terrible ordeal for him. He was not only unable to do anything for himself, but was also at times disorientated because of the drugs he was given and because of the lack of sensory input from his nerves.

When he came off the ventilator and had some movement of his limbs, he was very demanding towards Margaret. He would become impatient if she did not instantly attend to his needs, for example if his mouth became dry or his tracheotomy needed sucking out. She was happy to be of service to him, and was very patient with him. Though spending most of the time with him in the intensive care unit, she felt freer than before, because she had control of her comings and goings. Though she never missed a day, she did not have him interfering with her life.

The acute attack eventually subsided, and he was able to return home. After intensive rehabilitation, he recovered a certain amount of control of his limbs, but he remained partially paralysed. However, their relationship continued to improve, and their love for one another deepened.

Journal

Margaret and Shadow needed a sacrifice to restore their relationship; most relationships hopefully require rather less to keep them alive. I suppose I identify with Shadow, in that there are times at present when I feel that only some dramatic event like a terrible illness will bring Kathy and me together again. But such an extreme measure hardly bears thinking about.

Presumably, Shadow's feelings about death were connected to the loss of his mother, even though he had no conscious memory of her. Death had entered his life much too early on. Perhaps related to his loss was the fact that, until Margaret appeared, he had no conviction that he could sustain a relationship with a woman. It was as if he could not bear to lose a woman, so he made certain that he turfed them out before he became too heavily involved. Some people throw themselves into relationships and are prepared to face all the risks that follow; others are more cautious and only gradually give of themselves. Shadow was one of those who are both cautious and enclosed, and thus never fully live in the world, until his meeting with Margaret, which opened up new prospects.

Both Margaret and Shadow had early problems with mothering, which gave rise to difficulties in dealing with intimacy. Margaret's mother had left her just before she was adolescent, which must have had a profound effect on her development and her feeling about herself as a woman.

They were also both addicted to death—they could not find meaning in their lives without it being present in some way. Presumably, Shadow had early on in his life confused loss with death. It is difficult enough at the best of times to separate the two. We all have to come to terms with death sooner or later but it is difficult to adjust to life, and to put death in its rightful place, when death has been present so immediately from the beginning, blighting our subsequent life.

In a way, the death of Shadow's business partner gave him the opportunity to have real feelings about someone he cared for. The mixture of intense feelings at the funeral enabled him to be in touch with a more loving side to his personality, even though it became mixed up with death. Also, at the unconscious level, one could say that he was in a sense attending his mother's funeral and burying her. Yet, in another way, she came to life in the person of Margaret, the woman on whom he came to rely totally, at times like a helpless child.

Shadow's mother died soon after giving birth to him, possibly from suicide following post-natal depression. There is a link to my mother, in that she lost a baby before me. I was thus a replacement child, living in another's shadow ...

I had a strange dream last night, about my body being dissected. I was lying absolutely still, on a high, hard table. There were loads of other bodies in the room but, unlike me, all the others were covered with fresh sheets. A group of nervous medical students could hardly bear to view my dead, waxy flesh, my stiff limbs and staring eyes. At last, one jolly lass started hacking away at me with a sharp blade, exposing veins, nerves, and fat. I felt no pain, of course, as I was dead. Gradually, my body lost more and more parts. As I woke up, I had the thought that at least I was lighter. But then I thought of how the weight of my body gives Kathy pleasure when we make love, and I am on top of her.

A gruesome dream. Perhaps it relates to a fear of what I might find if I dissect myself and my marriage. Will there be nothing left? Also, there is the issue of how much of me, a whole or merely some small part, is alive to Kathy, and vice versa. The fact is, I feel almost nothing at the moment. My life continues, but I barely feel alive. Is this some stage through which I have to go, a kind of trial to make me stronger, or a test of my will?

I feel most alive now while struggling with my writing. The fear is that I put all of myself into this task, leaving nothing much in the real world, where I barely exist and yet have real responsibilities. Soon I may have to make a choice about whether or not I continue to write. I am driven to write, but I feel increasingly uncomfortable about what is driving me.

I conceived the next story as a series of letters, which requires a certain shift of reading perspective. I also have to admit that the form rather reflects the somewhat fragmented state of my world at the moment. As for the content, I suppose that it is not particularly pleasant, because it involves the personal exploitation of a young female patient of mine. I have used my experience of her in sessions to draw a picture of the male character. She often put me in the position of a potential exploiter, for example experiencing me as sadistic and remote, and out to humiliate her. I have also added to him some of my worst characteristics. An anatomy lesson perhaps; hopefully not yet a post-mortem.

Letters from a castle

November 2001,
Cambridge.

Dear Martha,

It is now a year since we last met, and you may wonder why I am writing to you now. In fact, I have been meaning to write to you for some time. I have even begun to do so on several occasions. But I have never been able to find the right words to convey my true feelings. I suppose I wanted to impress you with my elegance of style and breadth of thought. Now, at last, I have given up any idea of being precise or clever. I have spent so much of my life hiding behind my professional and professorial persona that I hardly know where to start when it comes to expressing my emotions. I am, as you know, a recluse. I prefer the safe solitude of my house in this parochial university town to the hazardous world of society. My lectures and supervisions are my main sources of social contact; in them, I feel momentarily alive, with all you young people paying attention to my words.

Otherwise, I am surrounded by walls, those outside and many within. It is perhaps of some significance that I have just had my front garden wall repaired and raised higher. It was beginning to crumble and was also low enough for passing school children to sit on. Now it is too high for them, and, furthermore, it is pointed on top and thus too uncomfortable to sit on.

You see how I spend my time—building defences against the world's intrusions. And yet I have decided to write to you a year after we met for our final tutorial. It was a very sad occasion for me, for I very much enjoyed our meetings. You have a fine mind, and I am sure you will succeed in carving out an academic career, should you so wish.

But why, you ask, do I choose to launch a letter from my castle? Perhaps you think that I do this to all my young female supervisees? Be assured that you are the first to whom I have written. I hope that I have not shocked you too much. It was not my intention.

I hear from Dr Peters that you are doing well. I am sure you know her, she is an expert in medieval history. She tells me that you are doing fine things with your book. If it is as scholarly as your thesis, then you will have no difficulty in finding a publisher and a public. If I can help in any way, feel free to ask. I have many connections in academic publishing. I gather that you are now interested in the transition period between the collapse of the Commonwealth and the restoration of the Monarchy. A strange and interesting time. As the old order collapses, you can see its essential elements more clearly as they fail to retain their hold on society. You can also begin to see what will then arise, in a kind of pure form, before the dust has settled and the bonds of society have become firm again.

Oh, if only I could leave my house and speak to you face to face. But even a phone call terrifies me. Please, never phone me. I do not know what to say, with the receiver close to my ear. It always gives me a terrible sense of loss. I want to reach out, but cannot. I want to say so much, but quickly dry up. I am acutely aware of the disembodied voice on the line waiting in vain for my replies. I have recently installed an answering machine. Before, I would let the phone continue to ring. Who knows, perhaps you have tried to call me?

I think a lot about death. What a dreadful phrase. Please do not put the letter down. Just hear me out, and then, if you tire of me, all you have to do is to ignore it. After all, that is the beauty of letter writing. You can simply refuse to answer, and our correspondence will end.

I live a strange kind of life, rarely socialising, living on a kind of knife-edge between living and dying. I am no longer in contact with my family. I believe that my brother, whom I have not seen in years, is living somewhere in the USA. I once had a wife, about whom I feel rather bad. I was not very nice to her. I do not mean that I was cruel or anything like that, and she knew the risk she was taking when she became involved with me. I just neglected her.

Why am I telling you all this? Surely I should try to impress you, not reveal my dark side. Perhaps I have already shocked you so much that you have decided to tear up my letter. I would not blame you if that is what you are doing. Indeed, I implore you now to do just that, before it is too late. I have already taken a terrible risk by writing to you. Your silence would relieve me of the anxious burden of continuing the correspondence.

You see how I live on the edge. One move on your part could make all the difference. If you throw away my letter, I shall continue as before. But if not, then …?

You must be angry with me by now, as I am imposing on you. At the very least, you may think that I should be locked away behind my high walls, as I am a menace to young women. You are absolutely right. But I am even more of a menace to myself. It may surprise you to know that I have had a number of "offers." That is to say, there have been attempts to reform me, naive hopes that I might change. There is nothing more deadly than a wish to change someone, believe me. I reacted badly, I provoked severe rows. I know I provoke anger, if others get too close to me—hence, no doubt, my safe isolation.

Before I give up completely on living in the social world, I want one last chance. Even I deserve that, surely? But I need some help. I hope that is not too much to ask of you. I will explain myself. I need a sort of bridge to the outside. In the past, I have tried to plunge myself right into the thick of things, but only met with disaster. Perhaps it would have been different if I had had an intermediary to smooth my path. I suppose it would be a bit too awful to remind you of all the help I gave you when I was your tutor. I am sorry. I stooped rather low for a moment. But rather than scrub out those offending words, I have decided to let them stand, so that you know my thoughts, however squalid. Having got this far, there is no point in practising a kind of censorship. I have done that far too often in the past.

What you could do for me is … how can I put it? Well, you can live for me, by telling me about your life. You can learn from my mistakes, see how not to conduct your life. And you can give me something to live for—I do not mean in some melodramatic sense. No, don't worry about that sort of thing.

This must sound all very odd to you, and yet it is very ordinary. I want to revel in your youth and vitality. Perhaps it is too late for me to find a way out of my castle. Perhaps the fortifications are too strong. Impregnable. Please at least give me a chance. Write to me. Keep in touch.

Yours gratefully,
P.B.

December 2001,
London.

Dear Professor B.,

Thank you for your letter, which I only received a week or so after you sent it, as I have been having a holiday in Paris. I thoroughly enjoyed myself there. The weather was generally satisfactory, though of course a little chilly. I was able to visit a number of exhibitions and museums, but the high point was a spirited performance of Carmen at the Paris Opera. People have criticised the building for being like a big loo, but I could not disagree more. It is full of light and space, the acoustics are excellent, and the atmosphere intimate. The only irritating thing was that a programme seller kept shouting, in a loud, high-pitched voice, "Programmes!," throughout the two intervals.

Well, what can I say about your letter, which of course came as a shock? I have to admit that I spent several hours in a state of confusion. I thought of contacting one of my friends, whom you also supervised, just to check on whether or not you had written to her. I did wonder if you did this kind of thing regularly, despite your assurances to the contrary. I will trust you, for the moment.

But I am still confused and also rather angry. What do you really want of me? You have put me in a difficult position. I cannot afford to antagonise influential people such as you. Did you write to me because I am vulnerable? It is difficult enough for a women to succeed in academic life. The positions of power are held by men. I neither want to play up to them nor alienate them. I just want to do my own work, which I know I do well, womanfully.

I must say that I never knew how much you have suffered. You hide your feelings very well. You always seemed to be quite together. I would never have imagined that you were shy, though you had a reputation for disliking parties. You were always relaxed with me. I really enjoyed our sessions; you never tried to force your opinions on me, but enabled me to think for myself. I feel sad about you now. It hurts me to hear how you really live. I thought that I had been close to you, professionally that is, but now I realise how much I did not see. Perhaps that is the price I pay for being immersed in old manuscripts. I, too, can isolate myself, though I also enjoy company.

I am not yet settled in my personal life. Until I have a more secure job, I am not sure what to do. My research fellowship has another two years to run, and maybe then I'll decide what to do, whether or not to buy a place, etc. I am renting a room in a flat of a woman friend. It's not spacious, but it's quite adequate for my current needs. But I really am confused about all sorts of things—myself, my career, my life.

Oh, dear, what am I saying? You asked for my help, and here I am spilling out to you. You were always kind to me. When I had some problem with an essay, you had a knack of letting me find the solution. You facilitated my thinking. That's quite a rare gift. Most other teachers are only interested in conveying their own ideas—they cannot bear anyone else's thinking, especially if they are a woman.

I hope my confusion has not frightened you. I am no longer so angry, but I am still suspicious of your motives in writing to me. I have to admit that I was flattered by your approaching me. I shall assume that I really am the only one. If you have done a mail shot (or, rather, a "male shot") to all your female ex-students, then I do not wish to continue our correspondence. I did, in fact, try to phone you but, as you said in your letter, all I ever got was the answering machine, and I just could not speak into it.

It really is difficult communicating in this way. Perhaps we have all lost the art of letter writing, thanks to the ease of picking up the phone. But then the phone, and now email, have saved an awful lot of misunderstandings. I feel that I am talking to the air. I thought I knew you, but I was obviously mistaken, which has left me rather disorientated. Well, shall I take up your challenge or not? What's in it for me? I could write an essay on the moral choice involved, but would that help me?

I am not used to disclosing myself to men. I am much more comfortable in the company of women. Of course, I like men. I went with one to Paris, but that is another story. You may be asking too much. You want me to describe my life to you, so that you may get vicarious satisfaction from me. That's an intrusion into my private life. A form of abuse. I am really surprised at you. Any kind of relationship, however distant, requires some sort of mutual disclosure. If I were to comply with your request, I would feel that you were always looking down at me, intruding into my thoughts and my imagination. I would have no freedom.

You must be very desperate, Professor. I would like to help you, but I am not sure it is possible—the terms are unacceptable. On the other hand, I sense the despair behind your request, and I do not want to turn my back on you.

In fact, you have found me at a difficult time in my personal life, at a crossroads. I am involved with a married man and, although I love him, I am uncertain whether or not I am doing the right thing. Would you be able to understand my dilemma? Frankly, from what you wrote about yourself, I would doubt that you had the experience to give any guidance. Yes, you see how desperate I am, too. Although I dislike revealing myself, I find myself opening up to you. Only, please do not take advantage of my distress.

I must end now. I have revealed too much. I hope you feel better about things. I will see how you respond before committing myself to paper again.

Yours sincerely,
M.D.

December 2001,
Cambridge.

My Dear Martha,

I had given up all hope of receiving a letter from you. I thought that you had been repelled by my appeal. It was with great relief that I read you had been away in Paris. Thank you so much for writing. I want to reassure you of my benign intentions. I do not wish to take advantage of your vulnerable position. I just do not know to whom I can turn. It sounds pathetic, doesn't it, a man of my age and experience with no one to whom he can truly turn for friendship or support? But it is true, none the less. I have no close family to look after me. My friends are all intellectuals. We have interesting conversations about history, politics and such like, but we do not share our personal suffering. That definitely would not do. Indeed, for many years I have believed that you should keep all that to yourself. I am like a crab with a hard, protective shell.

To illustrate what I mean, I want to tell you a dream I had the other night. There was someone, probably a woman, looking down on me from a great height. I become aware of my face, which feels like a lunar terrain, with great pits and craters. It feels as if I am being subject to constant bombardment. I feel like this woman's satellite, following helplessly the ebb and flow of her emotions. Pity me, I plead. I need protection. But I lack a protective layer and feel raw. Her look strips me to the bone. I turn into an edible crab with half-eaten limbs, trying to stir up the sand in a rock pool. "Leave me alone," I say, as I retreat into the small world of the crustacean.

Well, I am that miserable crab. I do not mean that in a self-pitying way. I am merely being realistic. I have not found a way of being close to people, and when I try I quickly retreat into the safety of my crevice. On the way, I lose the odd limb. It is only when I study, when I delve into the past and immerse myself in the richness of past lives, that I begin to feel whole. Do you know what I mean? I hope so.

I have revealed more to you than to anyone. I am at your mercy. Vulnerable. I swore I would never allow that to happen. I have enemies—who doesn't, especially in the rivalrous world of academia? I am not popular. More respected than loved. I am not generous to colleagues, perhaps out of fear of them. But neither am I narrow-minded or unnecessarily critical. When I do criticise, I respect the other's point of view, even when I think it to be erroneous. But if I find pretentiousness or a lack of scholarship, I am ruthless in my criticism. Like a crab, I am cold-blooded. Hardly the kind of creature to whom one can feel much warmth of feeling.

Yet I am not past all hope. I am sitting on a large green sofa on which I often rest, and which looks out onto my back garden. I find gardening a great relaxation. I am not one of those tidy types who loves to have neat rows of daffs and the like. I prefer a rather vivid and chaotic mixture of plants and their colours, though of course there is not much to see at the moment. I have a wide though not long garden, with a high back fence (what else would you expect?). On the fence, I have arranged several climbing plants, such as Clematis and Ivy, and they intertwine and cover the fence with their ever searching fingers.

I realise that I have not said how charmed I was by your letter. I would not have blamed you if you had dropped mine into the waste bin. That would have been a perfectly reasonable thing to have done. But I am glad that you did not. Very glad indeed. You have made me almost happy. I say almost, because, as you know, I cannot allow myself the pleasure of unmixed feelings, except perhaps when listening to music. I have spent many delightful hours on the sofa, giving my attention to songs and opera. Perhaps you thought I would only like cerebral music. While it is true that I gain an intellectual satisfaction from attending to a complex string quartet or a dense symphony, the human voice touches an area of myself that remains untouched and untouchable in the everyday world. Perhaps it is easier for me to feel alive in the safety of my castle. Yes, that is precisely the problem, for it means that I have little motivation to move out and to risk encounters.

I do not think much about my childhood. It was not a particularly interesting time for me. What a terrible confession to make in these dreadful post-Freudian days. What I do recall with some pleasure is the sound of my mother singing melancholy folk tunes. She came from a large family in the Outer Hebrides. She was glad to escape the enclosed island society but she missed the intense community life, and she conveyed her melancholy through song. Certain tunes still fill my eyes with tears.

I am a sucker for romantic opera, particularly that of Puccini. Of course, I also love Carmen. Maybe I will pop over to Paris to visit the Opera. It sounds most interesting. What was the Carmen like? I have seen it many times over the years, and it still grabs me in the guts. The image of woman as devouring and insatiable, able to bestow favours whenever she pleases, is fascinating and terrifying. As I gave up long ago any attempt to form a lasting relationship with a woman, Carmen's image perhaps holds fewer terrors for me than for other men who dream of more permanent possession. The notion of permanence seems like death to me. I have seen too many people who have wrecked their lives by imagining that a lasting relationship was possible.

I do have a vague yearning for such a thing from time to time but I soon feel better, and dismiss it from my mind as a passing aberration.

Now, to turn to what you wrote at the end of your letter, that you are involved with a married man. You doubt my capacity to help you. You are probably correct. What would I know of such things, being neither a woman nor a married man? It goes without saying that you must be in a mess. From what I have observed, marriage itself is a mess, so being near to it, even at one remove, brings with it all sorts of chaos. Some people like to take all that stuff on board, for being tied down to society's norms gives them a sense of meaning. For me, that only means being in contact with society's madness, its daft customs and institutions. Of course, I could be a lot happier were I to take such a daunting step. It would no doubt be a lot better than being stuck in my own private institution. Still, it's hardly likely.

The point is, my dear Martha, you have to ask yourself whether or not your affair is worth all the fuss and bother. Is a man worth it? Speaking as one, I think not. Also, make sure that you are not part of some game between him and his wife. He may be using you merely to boost his own self-esteem. I am sure you must have asked yourself these mundane questions, so forgive me for stating the obvious.

Well, I think I have said enough. I sincerely hope you will reply to my missive.

With hope and fondness, also have a happy Christmas (don't expect a present).

Yours etc,
P.B.

1st January, 2002,
London.

Dear Professor B.,

Thank you for your letter, which I enjoyed reading, and which was also a help. Do not be surprised or shocked. What you wrote at the end, in your throwaway manner, did actually help me to focus on what was essential. At first, I read your letter with mounting trepidation, because I thought you were going to ignore my personal problems. I was quite prepared for that. What you otherwise wrote reassured me about your intentions.

You revealed aspects of yourself that I would never have imagined. I was moved. The image of the crab seems terribly pathetic. Can that really be how you see yourself, or is it how you would like to see yourself? I apologise for my scepticism, but the image seems so far from the reality I experienced in your presence. But then I suppose we academics are good at putting an intellectual gloss over our personal difficulties. Our minds are a burden to us.

You are correct in saying that I am in a mess, perhaps more than you realise. I have had a miserable Christmas. Instead of planning Christmas Day to be with my family or friends, I spent it on my own, brooding on my situation and hoping that *he* would drop his family commitments and visit me. I cannot imagine what made me so naive. Christmas is for children. I could not expect him to leave them just for me.

The trouble is, we had such a good time in Paris. He managed to arrange a few days for us, supposedly on business. In a way, I had hoped it would be a disaster, and that we would be forced to end the relationship there and then. But life is not that simple. Well, at least my life is not. Complications always set in. Why, for example, did you choose to write to me, of all people? There must be something about me that attracts trouble. Am I easy prey? Do I set myself up to fail?

We stayed in a snug hotel in the Marais district. It was surprisingly quiet there, and full of charm. The only disquieting thing was the relative absence of women in the streets round about. It seems it was something of a gay area. There were one or two bars and cafés where, if you peered in, rows of anxious male faces met your gaze. They certainly do not have the sense of freedom that gay people enjoy in London, even with the prejudice they still suffer here. The Parisian men took themselves too seriously, they were not having a good time.

Well, that strange atmosphere was perhaps appropriate for Paul and me. We certainly enjoyed strolling around the streets, popping into exhibitions and feasting on the cuisine. But I was only too aware of the unreality of our situation. Paul, in contrast, is good at denying difficulties. He likes to enjoy the moment and to hope for the best, which I find both attractive and infuriating.

Once we were back in London and had to face the realities of his wife and children, even he could no longer pretend that all was well. I am supposedly an adult and knew all along what I was getting into. I suspect that I do not really want to commit myself to Paul wholeheartedly. You might say that was a good thing, and that in your experience total commitment is a dangerous illusion, especially at my age. I shall be thirty in a couple of years. I have given myself until then to have the main aspects of my personal life reasonably settled. Is that another pathetic illusion? There is nothing more unattractive than a desperate woman.

I have been invited to a New Year's party tonight. I am determined to have a good time, even if I drink several litres of wine in the process. I have been wasting too much of my life wallowing in self-pity. I shall take hold of myself and plunge into the thick of things.

I am sorry not to have told you about my work, but the fact is I am in rather a fallow patch. I have completed a rough outline of a paper concerning the early phase of the Restoration, where I consider how the old and new regimes intermingle, and how the strange mixture of the two still haunts us today. I do not yet have the impetus to flesh out the details. They will come in due course. Thankfully, I have reached the point with my work when I know that, given time and patience, something useful will appear. Only I get frustrated with the time it takes. This has been a scrappy letter. I hope you can make sense of it. I had better get changed for the party.

Yours etc.,
M.

January, 2002,
Cambridge.

My Dear Martha,

I hope that the party went well. I look forward to hearing about it. I hope it's not one of those ghastly gatherings of jolly academics. They always go over the top in an effort to enjoy themselves—it's terribly false.

What news from my castle? Well, something strange is happening. I feel as if I am gazing out from sleep through closed eyes, with my face flattened and pressed hard against fragile glass, which might shatter at any moment. I am asleep yet, from deep within me, a cluster of passions have begun to rise up. There is the fear of being blown apart. Can you understand me? Your letters touch me deeply. I begin to feel with you, as you describe your situation. Beneath my usual unmoving surface there are intermittent flashes of life.

I dreamed last night that I was in a boat, paddling through still waters. I came to a halt among some clear shallows. The contour of the shore was the shape of a woman's smile. The beach felt sensuous and inviting. I tried to get out of the boat but, as I did so, I began to sink into the lake, which became a mirror. I woke up feeling tremendously sad.

I have recently been tempted to leave my house and to meet you. You worry me. You are vulnerable and are being used by that fellow. My advice is to drop him.

Forgive me for that last paragraph. It was quite inexcusable. Your love life is none of my business. Still, I shan't delete it.

Do you understand my dream? I am all over the place. It is very disconcerting. I should omit these lines. You might take fright, or flight. Perhaps you see me as some kind of father figure to whom you can turn in time of need. I do not want to let you down.

I do not usually recall my dreams. Perhaps it is a sign of something stirring within. The lake that becomes a mirror— what to make of that? I have a horror of mirrors, and especially my reflection. I suppose it's obvious why—I do not wish to be reminded of how much I dislike myself.

Your life has become a pleasant mirror, an image of all the things I would have liked to have done. If only I had been in such turmoil over love, instead of avoiding intimate encounters. I have not put myself on the line, as you have done. I realise now, more than ever, that I have not been alive, except in the biological sense.

I feel ill. I have been wandering about all day in the house, not knowing what to do with myself. The weather is bad. The garden does not need work on it at the moment. I do not feel like listening to music. What am I to do?

I feel like an adolescent, or at least I think I do. I never had a full adolescence. I seemed to have skipped the usual developmental stages, the heartaches, and the passions. Instead, I was devoted to my studies. I did not seem to interest girls, and I never had the courage to ask them out. Of course, later on I did acquire experience with women, but too little, and with little affection. I will not shock you with the details.

I have just read over the contents of this letter, which I wrote over a couple of days. I come across as a gibbering idiot, but

I am loath to throw it away. Maybe you can see some sense. Perhaps there is a way to rescue me from the grave. I hope that my ravings have not frightened you. It just seems easier to express oneself on paper. The written word does not bite back. Knowing that you will read the words adds the element of anxiety. Please believe me when I say that you are the first to know my inner thoughts, let alone my dreams.

I look forward with trepidation to your next letter.

Yours ever,
P.B.

February, 2002,
London.

Dear Professor,

I apologise for the delay in replying to your last letter. As you can imagine, it came as something of a shock. Of course, as I myself revealed to you some intimate aspects of my life, it was reasonable for you to reciprocate. But you did somewhat overwhelm me. I do not know how I can help you—I am so preoccupied with my own problems. I was moved by your confessions. Your dream was vivid, but why did you tell it to me? Perhaps you should see someone who can understand them and help you. Maybe some kind of therapy would help. I am thinking of having some myself. Friends cannot help with everything.

By the way, I did enjoy the New Year celebrations. Actually, I don't remember very much of them, as I got through a fair amount of drink. I have decided that Paul is a bully. He only thinks of his own pleasures. He expects me to fit in with him. Of course, it isn't easy for him dealing with his children, but he uses them as an excuse to avoid confronting our situation. I came to this conclusion after the third glass of wine. I became convinced of it as the evening wore on. He is out to stifle me. My spirit will die if I continue with him. He has no intention of leaving his wife and children. Why do I get involved with men like him? He is not the first. I have to admit that I prefer older men, especially someone who is established. I suppose it makes me feel more secure—I do not have to compete with them, as I might have to with a contemporary. Is that silly of me? I want to look up to my partner, but I also want him to appreciate me. So many men, especially the younger ones, fail to consider women as ordinary human beings. They do not realise that making a woman laugh is much sexier than being macho.

I am off to Russia soon. A friend is organising a conference in Moscow to promote exchanges between Western and Russian scholars. It sounds a fascinating project, though I doubt that anything substantial will come out of it. The Russians probably need bread more than ideas, though they've always been hungry for culture. I will be away for a week or so.

Yours,
M.

February, 2002,
Cambridge.

Dear Martha,

You will find this brief letter waiting for you when you return from Russia. I do not particularly expect a reply. I am very disappointed in you. You do not really believe in that Freudian claptrap, do you? All that therapy bandwagon. I am afraid for your soul. I obviously made a great mistake in writing to you in the first place. I really could not care less about your squalid little affair with your married man. As for your feelings about older men, I cannot imagine that you are referring to me, as you are not specific. Did you really read my previous letter? You treated me with contempt. I am too angry to continue this letter, so I send it incomplete, but with all my disappointment.

Yours,
P.B.

February, 2002,
Moscow.

Dear Professor,

I have finally managed to find a stamp for this letter. Moscow is fascinating but chaotic. Business blooming everywhere. However, many of the professional people I mix with still despise businessmen and see them as criminals. No doubt there is some truth in this, with the Russian Mafia etc., but these Russians still have not got used to the notion of trade.

I am staying in a small flat with a female Russian colleague, in the living room. She sleeps with her husband and their four-year-old in one bedroom, her mother-in-law in the other one. Their living situation has become rather tense, because the grandmother and my friend disagree about childcare. The grandmother is too easy-going for my friend, who wants clearer limits for the child. They have occasional rows about this, even in my presence.

The conference has gone well. The Russians are keen on making links with Western scholars. They can listen for hours to papers and discussions. It is very tiring for me, especially since I have to follow through an interpreter, who sits at my side.

I have met a charming man, Boris, a professor. He is much more cultivated and open-minded than the usual English equivalent, despite having been cut off from the outside for so long. He is interested in all our developments and eager to exchange ideas. In fact, the Russians here have a lot to give to the West, even if they do not often believe it themselves. We study history, they have really lived it with every fibre of their being.

Boris has taken me sightseeing, to the Kremlin, Red Square, and so on. The cathedrals are really beautiful and are now being used. Religion has had a new lease of life—one set of illusions replacing another. The only really disturbing event was a day of meetings and demonstrations at Gorky Park by ex-soldiers, most of whom look like young boys. They look very angry at not finding work. Some extreme nationalist group could easily take them over.

I hope that this letter reaches you some time, preferably before I return to England.

Yours,
M.

March, 2002,
London.

Dear Professor,

I have just arrived back at my flat and have read your alarming letter, which has very much puzzled me. Why have you suddenly turned on me? It is very unfair of you. I did read your previous letter closely, and gave you my genuine response. You are obviously cruel at heart. I was sympathetic to you and your plight. Maybe I was a bit insensitive in that I was probably unaware of what you felt about therapy. But what you told me about yourself somewhat frightened me. I cannot give meaning to your life, only you can do that for yourself. It is foolish to think you can live through me, or that I can save you from your situation.

You must get out of your house, however difficult that may be. Please do not imagine I am inviting you here. I do not wish that on any account. I am sorry if I appear hard-hearted, but I do not have the emotional space for you. I have enough problems of my own. I miss Boris terribly. He is so alive. He has an optimistic spirit, despite his bad working conditions, the low pay, and the fight to sustain himself against all the die-hards.

Maybe it was a mistake to exchange letters. You allowed yourself to risk more than you were prepared for. Why am I making allowances? You were very rude. I no longer care what you might do to my career. I have to admit that, despite your assurances to the contrary, I was worried that you might use your power against me. Of course, I was also flattered by your attentions, and hoped that you might be able to help in some way. I even had a brief fantasy that I might be able to help you as a research assistant or something.

Now I am determined to stand on my own feet, both in my work and in my personal life. I shall get on with my life from now on. After all, this is not a rehearsal for life, it is the real thing. If you wait for things to happen, then it will all be over before you have truly lived. Obviously nothing can come of a relationship with Boris, but being with him was an important experience. Despite all his privations, he and his friends know how to live and laugh.

I do not know where this is all leading. There is no doubt a message for you in it somewhere. I will not write again, unless you specifically request it. And even then I am not certain it would be wise. I hope you manage to feel a little better about things. I am sorry if I have not lived up to your expectations. I could never be what you expected.

Yours,
M.

March, 2002,
Cambridge.

To M.D.,

By the time you receive this letter, if not before, you will have heard of my death. This may sound melodramatic—so be it. I can find no other way of starting this final letter. I do not apologise for my act. I have decided, in the cool light of morning, and after reading your last letter, which arrived this morning, to put into action last night's decision to empty a couple of bottles of drink and then to hang myself. I suppose I had to make a decision about myself at some point, and now I have.

Compared to many people, I am privileged. I have enough food and money. I do not have any mortal illness that I know of, save for the chronic and incurable illness called life, and I am not in any physical pain. What better time, then, than to end it all now, before I fall ill, before some cancer takes hold of me and wastes my body slowly and painfully.

I realise that I cannot possibly raise myself out of my predicament. I thought that hearing about your life might have induced a process of change in me, but instead it has only made my condition worse. I was lulled into the false hope that I was capable of living in the open sea, as it were, rather than in my tiny crevice.

Your letters have persuaded me that my hope was mistaken. I do not mean to land you with the responsibility for my suicide. No, that is mine alone and, indeed, it has been coming for a long time.

I should have realised that I was at my most vulnerable just as I began to feel more in touch with myself. Instead of bringing relief, it has brought unbearable pain. I began to know what I have been missing all these years, and that knowledge has become intolerable. I can think of no elegant way of ending this letter, and no fitting epigraph. I am about to take a few swigs of Russian vodka—appropriate in the circumstances, don't you think?

P.B.

Journal

Although the professor was pretty nasty to Martha, at least she came out of the situation transformed in some way. She became more independent as a person—she had dropped her married lover, and was determined about her career. There is a toughness about her, which is probably why the professor chose her as the confidante for his innermost obsessions, or rather the dumping ground for them.

You can put in a letter what is difficult to say in person, but the danger is that communication can become unreal, with the absence of face-to-face confrontation to test out thoughts and feelings more directly. Perhaps there was an innate risk that the letters could lead to the expression of more and more fantasy.

The professor's dreams revealed a fragile sense of identity, behind his professional persona. He hid his more human side, with the result that he shrivelled up as a man and felt like a crustacean. Yet he was also over-sensitive. He tried to retain a hard shell on the outside, which acted as a barrier against people, but he was over-sensitive beneath the shell. He lowered his guard briefly, but could not then deal with the consequences. He was aware of his own painful states, but was quite oblivious to anyone else's pain.

Martha was a little rejecting, though one could hardly blame her—she was not a therapist, used to listening to pathological outpourings. Presumably, his anger with her was his way of dealing with his increasing dependency on her, but he could not escape his self-loathing, and suicide was inevitable. Indeed, as he said, it had been coming for some years. What made it fairly unsympathetic was his wish to involve her in the act. However, it is often the case that suicide, far from being some heroic act of choice, is often done in anger, and is directed at someone in a very personal way. It gives those who are left behind the feeling that they have been intruded upon.

The professor was barely holding on to life. Such people are unattractive—one shuns them for fear of catching their sickness. I see myself in him in some ways. Psychoanalysts are reclusive, although we deal with people's most intimate thoughts and feelings. I suppose his scepticism about the permanence of human relationships is a kind of antidote to my own conviction of the centrality of long-term relationships, but it also reflects my doubts about my capacity to hold on to Kathy.

I note with horror that I have begun to have jealous thoughts about her. I feel more and more a monster like the professor. I feel there is another man. At first, he had no shape, but he has begun to assume a particular form. Unlike me, he is tall. He is not that handsome, but is certainly charming. He has curly hair, a broad, self-satisfied grin, and is at ease with women.

Perhaps I am possessive and over-controlling. For example, at parties I dislike being separated from Kathy for long, and so I soon seek her out. I thought it was because I disliked parties, but now I realise it is because of my fear of the "other man", as well as the wish to keep Kathy within my sights. I dislike the fact that she seems completely out of my control, that she is always out of reach.

Of course, men have traditionally controlled women—it is built into our culture. Although in the last few years women have been wanting more autonomy, they are still a long way from achieving it. It is so difficult knowing how to sort out men and women's competing needs. Some couples solve the problem by retaining traditional roles—after all, this solution has been going on for generations, and we still do not know if new solutions will fare any better. Others attempt to share roles more. Affairs, separations, a change of house or job, can all be attempts at redefining a relationship. I do not wish to be too gloomy about finding happiness but there are so many failures these days, so much heartache and uncertainty, with only occasional moments of joy. Or are we self-indulgent?

Why do we have to hurt one another so much? I suppose it is sometimes only through first taking action that we can begin to reflect on ourselves. No amount of talking can convince us of the reality of our feelings. Too often, we have to recognise them by first experiencing pain, separation and loss.

Disaster has struck. This Saturday morning, I suddenly felt that something was wrong. The kids were playing with their friends in the street. I realised that I had not seen Kathy for an hour or so. Eventually, I found her in the upstairs bathroom in a collapsed state, sobbing. At first, she would not look at me, nor would she explain what was wrong. As she is usually very much in control of her feelings, it was a great shock to see her suffering so much. Finally, she admitted that she felt she was going mad, that she had so many thoughts crowding in on her that she did not know what to do. At first, I was afraid that this was all related to me, that she did not want to be with me, and that she was having an affair. She said that none of these fears were true. She explained that she has been under so much stress at work that she feels she can no longer cope. She feels that she needs more time for herself to sort things out, but she does not know how.

I feel that I have not given her enough time and attention, and offered to devote more time listening to her work problems. She eventually calmed down, and spent the rest of the morning doing the housework, as a way of diverting her mind from her problems. She felt better that night, but the next day the pressure built up again. As a result, she had an overwhelming desire to get out of the house and to be on her own. She drove off, taking the mobile phone with her. I was worried about her safety, in case she might kill herself or have an accident. She assured me that she would be safe. We had some anxious hours waiting for her call. It was difficult explaining away her disappearance to the children. She finally returned in the early evening, having driven around various parts of London while thinking about how to make sense of her situation. She was in therapy some years ago. She might go back to it.

I write about a week after these events happened. The situation seems calmer, but we are living on a knife-edge, afraid of what might happen next.

Partly as an escape from my troubles, I have thought up a story based on the treatment of the mother of an adolescent girl who fell in love at a holiday resort in Italy, creating all sorts of trouble for her family. I think we all need a holiday, but unfortunately there are some months to go before the summer.

Generations

The main setting for my story is a mountain village in the Italian Alps, in northern Italy. It is a picturesque little place, unspoilt by locust-like tourists, consisting of a small number of permanent residents who make a living from the land, or travel to work down at the coast, often in the flower business. A few residents also make their money from tourists in the summer season, when the village swells in size with those who have family connections. In addition, a few English people, and one or two Germans, have bought small properties in and around the village.

Just outside the village there is a picturesque old water mill, which was originally used for making bread out of chestnuts. It is no longer in use, but has been converted into a holiday home. A remarkable old lady, Sophia Grantwood, had been its owner for some seventeen years. She had been the first English person in the village, and was treated by the locals with great respect. She was small yet imposing, with a large head, aquiline nose, piercing blue eyes, and an energetic body. Her age was a well-kept secret, but she had been a grand old English lady for some years. She was well-off, partly because of inherited family income, and partly because her husband had left her a considerable amount of life insurance money following his tragic death in a road traffic accident just after the war. Sophia raised her only child, Gemma, on her own.

Soon after her father's death, when she was five, Gemma developed severe asthma, which at times was life-threatening. Although as an adult she managed to control her attacks, she needed continuous medication. Her constant wheeziness gave her a somewhat anxious and tight appearance. However, like her mother, she had a forceful personality. She trained as a doctor, specialising in skin conditions and allergies. Her husband, Alex, was a tall, good-looking and gentle man, who had his own successful design company. They had two children, Jenny, an outgoing and precocious fifteen-year-old, and Tim, a shy but pleasant eleven-year-old.

Sophia, the grandmother, called herself an artist. She did have a certain flair for colour, and produced pleasant, although unoriginal, impressionistic landscapes of the Italian and English countryside. Because they were pretty and reasonably priced, they sold well. It was in Italy that she most indulged herself in her fantasy of being an accomplished artist. On the door of her studio at the mill, she placed a plaque describing herself as "Sophia Grantwood, *artista*." She organised exhibitions of her work in the village hall, which were well-received and financially lucrative. Whether the villagers knew no better, or were just being polite, she was held in great respect as an imposing English lady artist, particularly because she appeared to be both wealthy and stingy. The locals respected the fact that she haggled with them over every item of expenditure.

The amenities of the mill were fairly primitive. Sophia had a penchant for the untouched and unsophisticated. There was no bath or shower, but plenty of portable bidets. The plumbing was antiquated and the plaster on the walls often crumbled. She spent just enough money to prevent the surrounding vegetation from taking over, although not enough to plug the many holes in the walls, so that scorpions and rats occasionally entered through them and dashed across the stone floors to frighten guests and tenants.

Although Sophia and Gemma had a rather fraught relationship, Sophia was deeply fond of her grandchildren, particularly the fifteen-year-old, Jenny. She was a bright girl, seemingly destined for university and a good career. She applied herself seriously to her work, and was often at the top of her class in many subjects. She seemed quietly self-confident. There was something very determined about her, which some people found a little uncomfortable, perhaps because she had a streak of that ruthlessness which was more obvious in her grandmother. Jenny could twist Sophia round her little finger. The girl could do no wrong in her grandmother's eyes. Sophia was fond of Tim. He was faithful and dogged, but lacked his sister's sparkle.

The family were taken by surprise one Easter when Alex ran off with his secretary, a much younger woman, who it turned out was expecting their baby. Gemma was shocked but rallied well. The children were miserable for some time, because they were very attached to their father, who had taken a major role in child-rearing. Jenny and her father had always had a close and affectionate relationship. When he left, she felt let down and very angry, and she refused to see him for several months. Tim was more forgiving, and continued to see his father regularly.

There was no attempt at a reconciliation. Alex made it clear that he had not been in love with Gemma for some time, and that he was happy with his new relationship. The separation and divorce were soon set in motion.

That summer holiday, Gemma took Jenny and Tim to stay at the mill with their grandmother.

Young people in the village, both native and summer visitors, tended to congregate in a small square, where they stood around, chatting, smoking or taking turns to ride a small motorbike. They also lounged about at a dingy bar and pizzeria, the Bar Dante, where they could sip drinks, play a video game, and listen to music from a jukebox, while watching the adult world go by, without much interference.

Jenny soon drifted into the Bar Dante. She spoke a little Italian, but most of the young people had a smattering of English, thanks to school and American movies. Though not a beauty, Jenny had sex appeal. Her curly brown hair was tied at the back, which drew attention to her pretty face, which was long and full with clear blue eyes. She carried herself with confidence, often smiled, and clearly enjoyed the interest she aroused.

Sophia was more concerned about Jenny's welfare than Gemma. The latter had rather given up imposing discipline on Jenny since the separation. Sophia felt that it was not her job to stand in for the mother, and was distressed that Gemma was opting out of being an effective parent. Sophia warned Gemma that the crowd at the Bar Dante were untrustworthy, and that it would not be long before some boys tried to take advantage of Jenny. Gemma accused Sophia of being an old-fashioned prude. She believed that Jenny had to find her own way of doing things, even if that meant her making a few mistakes. Sophia heartily disagreed with this attitude, for she felt that she might make any number of disastrous mistakes before she was mature enough to know what was in her best interests. Gemma refused to budge in her attitude and anyway, she argued, Jenny was not going to listen to what either of them said.

Very soon, a pack of predatory young men gathered around Jenny. She was especially attractive to them because she was a foreigner, someone out of the ordinary, and very different from the local girls, who were well-known and lacking in mystery. The fact that she was also from London added immensely to her status, for all the young people wanted to hear about what was going on there. It seemed to them the fascinating and romantic centre of the pop world, with so much more to offer than their narrow provincial environment.

One or two of the older men, in their late twenties, also congregated around the Bar Dante, mainly in the evenings, to drink, play cards, and chat up the young women. They were soon drawn to Jenny who, of course, was flattered by their attentions.

One of these men, Toni, appeared to be the leader of the group. He worked as an assistant to the local builder. He was heavily built, and had a rather boy-like smile and sense of humour. Enjoying his dominant position, he walked with a confident swagger, often teased the younger men about their inexperience with girls, and was proud of being able to take his drink. Only his sad brown eyes revealed a more vulnerable side to his nature.

He was immediately fascinated by the English girl. He bought her drinks, flattered her by praising her appearance, and emphasised her superiority to the local girls. He often asked her about England, a country he loved. He had once spent a few weeks in London, helping out a friend at a sandwich bar, as a result of which he was able to speak some colloquial English. He had always wanted to return to London, perhaps even to settle there, particularly since there were few prospects in the village and the neighbourhood. He was helping the local builder for the moment, but in time he wanted to set up his own business. Only, he added, times were difficult, with unemployment everywhere. You had to have capital. He was saving up what he could. He just needed time and a bit of luck to fulfil his potential.

When Toni discovered that Jenny was Sophia's granddaughter, he suddenly turned up at the mill in order to offer his services to Sophia. He did some minor repairs, shifted some logs, and cleared out a *cantina* full of rubbish. He was an open and friendly fellow, and easily managed to make himself useful. He was also cheap, which endeared him to Sophia. When she organised a barbecue for her English friends, Toni somehow managed to turn up in order to cook some trout for them. But she had been unaware of the developing friendship between him and Jenny. It was only at the barbecue that the truth became plain to her, for she observed how tender he was to Jenny, and how she kept smiling knowingly at him.

When the party broke up, Sophia noticed that Jenny and Toni had disappeared. She expressed her concern to Gemma, who shrugged her shoulders as if there was nothing she would or could do about the situation. Gemma made it clear that if that was what Jenny wanted, then it was fine by her. But even Gemma became alarmed when Sophia explained that Toni was married and had a three-month-old daughter. Furthermore, the wife was Sicilian, and if her brothers found out that Toni had been playing around with another woman, all hell would break loose. She doubted whether Jenny herself would be hurt, but she added that you could never be certain.

Gemma decided to hunt for Jenny, and went down to the village to make enquiries about her. The Bar Dante crowd knew nothing, but Gemma realised that if they did know they were unlikely to say. The other bars and shops were closed, and she drew a blank from other villagers she met.

Eventually, Jenny turned up at the mill, at three in the morning, to find her mother and grandmother waiting up for her.

"Where have you been?" said Sophia. "We've been worried sick about you."

"It's almost daytime," said Gemma wheezily.

"I've been out."

"But where?" Sophia insisted.

"Do stop nagging, nan," said Jenny mildly.

Sophia softened for a moment. "I was worried about you, dear. We both were."

"I can see you've ganged up on me."

"It's that Toni, isn't it?" said Sophia, her anger building.

"What if it is?" replied Jenny defiantly.

"I have to think of my relationship with the village. I really don't want a scandal."

Jenny laughed loudly. "Oh, come off it, nan. They don't mind."

"They are old-fashioned here," Sophia pointed out. "And he has a wife and baby."

"He told me," Jenny replied calmly. "He has been honest with me."

"You're so bloody naive," said Sophia angrily. "And you're much too young."

"No I'm not."

"He's just using you."

"He was forced to marry. He doesn't love her. He never has. He hardly stays there."

"And what about the baby?" said Sophia, holding up her hands in horror.

"Stop getting at me," Jenny replied with irritation. "Just leave me alone!" She then stormed off and locked herself in her bedroom.

"I think you pushed her too much," said Gemma. "She can be very stubborn. It's best to leave well alone for a while."

"Oh, that's typical of you, Gemma. Turn a blind eye. That's why you lost Alex."

"Oh, I've had enough!" replied Gemma angrily. She also stormed off, leaving her mother to brood on the evening's events in solitude.

Sophia sat for a while, distraught, regretting her lack of tact. She wondered if Gemma were right, and that coming down heavily on Jenny might be counter-productive. She was a stubborn girl, who would do what was bad for her just to spite everyone. Although in general a tolerant person, Sophia had rather strict sexual morals, perhaps not surprising in a person of her generation. She was also afraid that her own standing in the village would be adversely affected, and that she would be blamed for her granddaughter's misbehaviour. The local girls might well play around but they were more discreet about it, while Jenny was blatant.

Sophia's respect in the village was such that she was greeted by everyone, regularly entertained with meals, and accepted as an honorary Italian. Once the scandal broke, she feared that she would be shunned and would lose her precious reputation. However sorry people would be about her unfortunate predicament, they would put up barriers and ban her from their hearts. It seemed all too much for her to bear. She fretted away the night with such anxious thoughts, and gave up trying to sleep.

In the morning, she tried once more to persuade Gemma to take a firm line with Jenny, but to no avail. Gemma refused to intervene, because she felt this was an adolescent crush that would soon pass. It was not to be taken seriously, and if it were, that would only provoke Jenny into thinking it was more than a fling. She felt it was best to be patient and let Jenny have her bit of fun, for she was a bright girl and he was a labourer. She firmly believed that nothing would come of their liaison.

Sophia remained unconvinced by Gemma's reasoning. She felt that, with her father off the scene, Jenny was vulnerable. She was too young to know what was best for her, and could easily find herself being exploited. But Sophia soon gave up trying to persuade Gemma to take action, and she felt bitterly angry with her. She could not really be angry with Jenny, because she was too young to know her own mind. Indeed, she felt sorry for her and tender towards her.

When, eventually, Jenny woke up, at midday, Sophia tried a softer approach with her. But although Jenny was willing to listen and appreciated her grandmother's concern for her, she was unwilling to stop seeing Toni.

Toni, meanwhile, somehow managed to negotiate time off work, and spent most of the day with Jenny. They sat together alone and in company at the Bar Dante, and swam in the cool mountain streams outside the village. There was no mention of his wife and child. Nor were they to be seen in the street.

To her relief, Sophia did not experience any change of attitude towards her. She wondered if the villagers were hoping that the affair would end once Jenny returned to England. No doubt they imagined that Toni was having a holiday romance and would soon, in the winter, see sense and look after his family. He had always had a reputation for being a bit of a lad. Indeed, people were surprised when he married, and suspected that he was indeed forced into it by his wife's family.

Sophia was immensely relieved once Jenny, Tim, and Gemma left for home, and she herself could at last return to her painting, which she had been unable to pursue because she had been so fraught with anxiety about Jenny. Toni returned to his labouring job, and Sophia hoped that Jenny would soon forget him.

The only thing that troubled her about the affair was that Jenny had shown little distress at leaving. Sophia expected at least a few tears. Instead, Jenny was light-hearted, and thanked her grandmother profusely for the delightful holiday. The reason for Jenny's good humour soon became evident when Sophia herself returned to London—Toni had come over and was staying at Gemma's house. He had left his wife, and had no intention of returning to her. He described her as a nag, and added that he had never been happy with her. She was also totally under her family's thumb. Indeed, as soon as Toni left her, she returned to her parents' house. Toni said that he was not worried about what her brothers might do to him. He insisted that he could take care of himself, and that they would not dare to take him on.

Gemma accepted Toni's presence in the house. She encouraged him to look for work, which he did half-heartedly. Instead, he spent most of the time lounging about the house, occasionally doing the odd job, but mainly being with Jenny. She had just reached sixteen and had started her A-level course. However, she devoted little time to her studies as she was now besotted with Toni. She introduced him to her friends, but he did not mix well with them, partly because of his poor English, and partly because he was a fish out of water. So Jenny and Toni tended to keep to themselves. Anyway she felt more mature than her peers, due to her relationship with an older man. Her friends found Toni interesting at first, but after a while the novelty wore off, and they soon thought him merely pathetic. Jenny, however, found his naive optimism about his future in London endearing. She felt motherly and protective towards him, which somehow compensated for the difference in their ages. Indeed, he soon became very dependent on her.

Tim did not care much for Toni, but he was a boy who kept his feelings to himself. He tried to keep out of his way as much as possible.

Needless to say, Sophia was horrified at what was happening to her family. She had been upset by Gemma's separation—she was fond of Alex and genuinely sorry not to have much contact with him. But then to see him replaced in her daughter's house by what she referred to as a "lazy gigolo" was utterly humiliating to her. His continued presence in the house made it impossible to visit her family there. Instead, they had to come to her place, without, of course, bringing Toni.

Sophia could not hide her feelings of outrage from Gemma, whom she blamed for the situation. However, she did her best not to alienate Jenny, whom she still saw as the foolish victim.

As the weeks and months passed, there was no sign of Toni's leaving. He briefly found work as a waiter in an Italian restaurant, while Jenny managed to get down to her studies. By this time, they were sleeping in the same bedroom.

Sophia tried appealing to Alex for support but he, too, was helpless to influence events, since Jenny still hardly talked to him. He also reasoned that the more he disapproved of Toni, the more likely she was to continue the relationship, if only to spite him. She still had not forgiven her father for leaving the family—indeed, Alex wondered whether her involvement with Toni was designed to pay him back for going off.

Later in the year, Sophia suffered a minor stroke, during which she fell down the stairs of her house and was poorly for some days. The family rallied round her. Gemma came to stay until she was stronger. She was left with a slight weakness on one side, and some memory problems. From that time on, she had occasions when she would forget what she had told people. But because she was around her eightieth year, this difficulty appeared consistent with her age, and her audience would make allowances. It was, however, distressing to her as she had, until then, been in full command of her faculties.

While convalescing, Sophia spent some time thinking over Jenny's situation, and how it was going to change her own life in the village. For many years, she had looked forward to her weeks at the mill. She always felt replenished after painting and sketching in the countryside around the village, and along the winding rock-lined rivers of the area. She had almost become a natural part of the landscape. The imposing English lady artist was to be seen everywhere, striding along with her large white hat bobbing up and down, sketch book in hand. But now, all that had changed. She dreaded returning to the village. What had been a source of comfort had now become a source of shame. A mother and a baby had been abandoned. It was too terrible for words.

Sophia decided to act. She felt that her illness had been a warning to take her life more easily. Ever since her husband had been killed, she had driven herself hard in order to raise Gemma. Now, she felt that keeping on the mill was too much of a burden. She had to organise lettings, see to repairs, haggle with workmen, and make sure it was reasonably secure and tidy. There was always something to worry about. She felt that it was time to share that worry with her family. She had left the mill to Gemma in her will. But, apart from staying in it every couple of years or so, Gemma had not offered her mother any help with its running. So Sophia decided to call a large family meeting that summer, in order to discuss the mill's future. She included in her invitation several nieces and nephews, who had visited the mill from time to time. She hoped that between them all they could come up with a plan to ease the burden on her. Perhaps she also wanted to show the village that she took her family responsibilities seriously, despite the business with Jenny and Toni.

Toni continued to live at Gemma's house. He had been genuinely upset by Sophia's illness, and had wished to visit her but on no account would Sophia let him near. When the summer holidays came round again, Toni gave up his waitering job, and Jenny returned to the village with him, to stay in his mother's house. She had been a widow for several years. Toni was a dutiful son, openly affectionate to her and respectful. His mother was not happy that he had left his wife. On the other hand, she liked Jenny, and thought that she was more worthy of her son than his Italian wife, who was a poor provincial girl with little education.

Toni and Jenny fitted into the village's summer population with little difficulty. They once more frequented the Bar Dante, and his friends were glad to have him back. He made much of his English experience, exaggerating his success and showing off the language he had acquired.

Jenny in turn had learned enough Italian to speak reasonably well with the locals. This added to the favourable impression she had made on his mother, and also made it easier for others in the village to accept her. Meanwhile, his wife and child had returned with her mother to Sicily. Although she had lived in the north for some years, his wife was treated with a degree of suspicion still accorded to southern Italians in the north. Her place of origin diminished the hostility that might otherwise have come Jenny's way for having displaced her.

Meanwhile, the mill gradually filled to overflowing with Sophia's family, who had come from various parts of England to attend the big pow-wow. There were children of all shapes and ages, a couple of unmarried nephews in their early thirties with their girlfriends, as well as cousins and their partners. Accommodation was found in the village for some of them, but the bulk of the family encamped at the mill, with the help of mattresses and sleeping bags. The children found the whole event immensely exciting for they stayed up until late at night, and were subject to little discipline, as the adults talked and entertained one another.

However, it was not long before tempers became frayed and arguments broke out. The reason for this was that it was impossible to find common ground between Sophia and her family. For example, it was generally agreed among the relatives that the mill desperately needed modernising. But Sophia strongly and vociferously held the view that the whole of its rustic charm rested on it remaining essentially untouched.

There was deadlock. The relatives felt that Sophia was not serious about wanting help with the running of the mill. Her notion of receiving help was to be in total control of everything, rather than to share responsibilities. For her part, Sophia felt that the relatives were not seriously attached to the mill, and showed no genuine love and affection for it. She was particularly angry with Gemma for not offering to take charge of its upkeep. Sophia became increasingly bad-tempered with everyone, so that, after a few days, the others gave up trying to negotiate with her, and decided to enjoy the rest of their holiday. Sophia was both annoyed at their attitude and triumphant at having got her own way, even though it was probably not in her best interest to keep control of the mill.

Jenny took little part in the meetings. Although the only other member strongly attached to the village, she had no interest in the mill. Furthermore, there was no way that Sophia was going to leave it to her as long as she was with Toni.

By the end of the summer holidays, Jenny and Toni had found a small, dilapidated flat for themselves in the village. Even Gemma was worried about her taking such a major step at her age. But Jenny would not listen to her objections. She said that she could continue to work for her exams there, especially as the school in London was so chaotic that she had to teach herself most things anyway.

Toni was happy. He did up the flat very nicely, and was proud of his English girl, who increased his status with his mates. Jenny was also happy, and liked to walk arm in arm with him through the village. Although she had little in common with his friends, she liked being with him in their company, where he was treated with respect and a little awe.

When Sophia returned to England, she was afraid that, any day, she would hear that Jenny was pregnant. Although Jenny had already assured her that she had no intention of having a baby yet, Sophia was convinced that Toni would persuade her to go through with it, in order to keep her with him. Sophia also brooded for some time on the sterile family get-together. The more she went over it, the angrier she became. She did not acknowledge how difficult she had been—she felt that at her age she was entitled to have her own way over the mill's upkeep. She felt that her family did not treat her with due respect. Not only had she been shamed by her granddaughter, now the rest of the family held her in contempt. No doubt they were waiting for her to die, when they would inherit her money and property.

In order to spite them all, she decided to sell the mill secretly. She felt that there was little point in keeping it on now that her reputation in the village was tarnished. It must be said, however, that in reality most of the village accepted Jenny, and continued to hold Sophia in high esteem. But for her, life there was no longer an attractive proposition. She constantly dreaded bumping into Toni, and she no longer had the inspiration to paint there. Perhaps her changed feeling about the place was also the result of the stroke. It had certainly slowed her up and made it difficult to undertake long journeys, let alone walk along steep mountain paths. Perhaps, too, the stroke had exaggerated her natural cantankerousness. Whatever the reasons for her change of attitude, she soon found a buyer, an American film director who was living with his family in London and was delighted to obtain such a picturesque and substantial property in Italy. Needless to say, he modernised the mill, while retaining its charm.

Gemma was annoyed that her mother had gone ahead with the sale without her knowledge, but because she had little real interest in the mill she was also relieved that it was off their hands.

As for Jenny and Toni, their relationship appeared to go well for another year or so. Then she briefly returned to England to take her exams, which she passed with flying colours. But when she returned to the village, she found out that Toni had been playing around with another woman. Although he tried to make amends for his impulsive action, Jenny could not forgive him. She felt betrayed and attacked, after all the sacrifices she had made by leaving her country and family to live with him. He tried to persuade her that she was his only true love, and that the other woman meant nothing to him, but to no avail. She woke up with a start from her Italian dream and returned home, wiser although, happily, not embittered. She obtained a place at university, where she studied psychology.

Journal

As the author and, as it were, father of this story, I am relieved that Jenny at last saw sense, even if it was because of Toni's unsurprising misconduct. I assumed that sooner or later he would have another fling. He was the kind of man who would be unlikely to see what was wrong about that. I just was not certain when the truth would dawn on Jenny, and at what cost. I should explain that I do not have much control over what happens in these stories. I have to follow where I am taken by the way that the characters relate to one another.

Like Sophia, I had moments when I could have strangled the Gemma character (based on my patient) for her laissez-faire attitude, which is the worst kind of opting out of parental responsibility. I had to do a lot of work with the real Gemma over that issue, during her analysis.

Poor old Sophia. She had to be both grandmother and mother at her advanced age. Of course, she was a bit of a tyrant, and hardly easy to live with. It was not then surprising that Gemma was asthmatic, fighting for control over her breath, as she must have fought to retain any independence and control over her life as a whole against the will of a forceful mother. Maybe, in these circumstances, her laid-back attitude was her only means of survival. Mind you, it is possible that Gemma's attitude to Jenny was the wisest one in the long-term. After all, Jenny did leave Toni of her own free will. All along, she was determined to do what she wanted—the more she was opposed, the more determined she became to make her own choices. However, she was also getting at her father, with whom she was furious for abandoning the family. The whole father issue was played out with Toni. One could also argue that if Gemma had been a more effective parent and had been able to tolerate Jenny's anger about the divorce, then the affair would have soon petered out. There were unconscious motives that made it difficult for Gemma to intervene in the situation effectively. It was perhaps her revenge on her ex-husband and, also, on her own father, who had died young. All around there were absent or abandoning fathers—Toni himself left his wife and baby for Jenny.

The three generations in Jenny's family were in constant interaction. The story began with the trauma of the grandfather's death, which left Sophia having to cope as a single parent with Gemma. Jenny was both looking for a father in Toni, a much older man, but she was also attacking her father, because Toni was an anti-father figure, the polar opposite to her own father. The moment that Toni was unfaithful, as her own father had been, she dropped him. Somewhere, she must have sensed that this might happen eventually, given the apparent ease with which he had left his wife and child. In the meantime, Jenny also matured, while Toni remained emotionally a little boy. Perhaps that difference was bound to lead to their break-up at some point. Indeed, Toni's impulsive action at the end could have been his way of trying to assert his independence from Jenny, who was becoming too powerful for him.

Jenny perhaps reminds us that it is never easy becoming an adult. Some of us never quite make it—we prefer to remain adolescent. Unfortunately, there are many older people who do not forgive adolescents for being on the threshold of a new life—they take their revenge by exploiting them. Others just skip through adolescence as fast as they can, becoming old before their time.

My own adolescence was pretty confusing. I could hardly talk to girls, although I thought about them the whole time. This was in part a consequence of attending an all-male day public school, where girls were the butt of smut, rather than potential partners in mutual enjoyment. Thankfully, this sorry state changed when I left home for university and then fell in love with an American student of literature, an older woman. She was generous and warm-hearted, and initiated me into sex. She also liked the poems I wrote at that time, which does not say much for her literary judgment. I really missed her when she returned to the States, but we lost contact.

God, I hated school, even though I did well. I was very intense. I recall a teacher's report in which he described me as someone who would not allow a second to be frittered away in frivolity. I have not changed. I must be a nightmare to live with. That teacher also described how I would sit at my desk nervously, hunched up in anxious anticipation that something beyond my control was going to occur and destroy my secure position. No, nothing has changed. I am still hunched up at my desk, now that I am writing these stories.

Kathy gave me a rare (these days) affectionate kiss this morning, which made me feel sad. I was suddenly aware of what I had not given her, all the lost moments. I thought of the many hours I have spent in my consulting-room, seeing patients and, now, writing, more of which I could have spent with her. It might only have been an hour here or there. Then the hours mount up, making weeks, months and then years of lost time.

If Kathy and I were to separate, the prospect of solitude fills me with dread, and yet I suppose I would cope. It is a ruthless fact of life that men of my age find it easier to rebuild their lives than women do. A number of my male friends have already done so, although that is no reason to wish for it. In the story "Letters from a Castle," I described, in however a distorted form, the power of the older man over the younger woman. One may wonder quite why Martha capitulated to him at first. Was it out of fear, or from ambition, or from some deep wish for security? Some women prefer an older man, not only because of the need to be looked after by a kind of father figure, but also because there is often less rivalry with him, particularly if he is already established professionally. Kathy and I have been together since our twenties, and so we have had to support one another as we were carving out careers. That has been a fruitful part of our relationship, but there has also always been a certain amount of professional rivalry between us. Indeed, I wonder how much of our present difficulties stem from the fact that I am now established, while her job is giving her grief.

Of course, there are dangers if a relationship remains static. Partners have to grow in their own way, hopefully in tandem and as a result of their relationship. But the partnership has to be able to encourage, or at least withstand, change. Clearly this is a preoccupation of mine. I wonder how much I am resisting change in my marriage, and how much Kathy's distress is a reaction to my wish to keep things the same. She now says that she wants more independence. Although I know intellectually that this is probably a good thing, I am worried about it. I am scared that this means she wants to leave me, or that we will no longer have the same degree of intimacy. She has begun to go out more with her own friends. I hope that this is not a disguise for an affair. I have been tempted to hire a private detective to follow her, but I must control my suspicions and trust her. Even if she is having an affair, the truth will eventually come out. She will tell me, or find some way of letting me know.

Sometimes I despair when I realise how much I want to hold on to what I have, or have had, and which even now I may be losing. When I think of change, my immediate image is of being in a bog, unable to move. Yet I know, from observing other people's lives, how suddenly things can be swept away, which is perhaps why I cling so desperately to what I think I have. Yet holding on to something too tightly causes despair and the risk of crushing what you have.

Meanwhile, I have come up with another story. I am rather ashamed of my writing impulse, especially since this next story had in part been inspired by my experience of Kathy's distress, as well as that of one of my patients who became depressed after the birth of a baby. Partly out of shame, and partly to disguise the identity of my patient, I have decided to place the events of the story in the fairly distant past, in the Victorian age. Maybe it feels a lot safer for me to imagine events then. But, in addition, I have always been attracted to people and events at that time. My father came from a once well-to-do family that made its money in the great era of Victorian expansion, but which then lost it all in the Great

Depression of the 1920s. He always had a yearning for his family's past glories, which has affected me. I like researching my patients' past. Indeed, I sometimes feel like a historian looking for clues from the past to account for the present. In order to bring the past to life, I have chosen to tell my story through the eyes of an imaginary young woman, and in the form of a diary.

Diary of a Victorian lady

Imagine this young woman, Mabel Hope, to be about twenty years old. She was a friend of another young woman, Lady Mary Y., a mother of three young children. Mabel joined her friend for the summer period, as Lady Y. was not feeling well. She had recently lost a baby soon after birth, and her spirits were low. Her husband, Lord William Y., a wealthy landowner, not much older than her, did not spend much time with his family because his estates and banking interests in London took up much of his time and energy.

Mabel kept a revealing diary of her summer with the family, from which I have, as it were, selected certain passages. It begins as Lady Mary, her children and Mabel arrive at Lady Mary's London residence, before leaving for her estate in Sussex.

7th July, 1891.

Feel rested at last. I had a good night's sleep. But Mary contin-ues to look troubled. If only she would speak to me. I have tried to be available to her. After all, she did ask me to spend the summer with her, as she felt so rotten after her baby died. Poor thing. William is apparently not much help.

93

Mary looked a little better in the evening, but did not talk much. Went to bed early.

8th July.

Mary came to my room in the middle of the night in a terrible state. She looked like something out of Walter Scott's Bride of Lammamoor, or like Mrs Rochester. Her face was pale, her hair was all over the place, and her nightgown was dishevelled. She clutched at me in despair, while her eyes seemed to be focused on somewhere far away.

"What on earth's the matter?" I asked anxiously.

"I couldn't sleep. I haven't had a peaceful night for ages."

I offered her some brandy, which she took eagerly.

"Oh, when will it stop?" she said wearily.

"But what is it?" I asked again.

She held my arm, and, with flowing tears, repeated over and over: "It's the child, the child."

I tried to comfort her, and eventually she calmed down a little.

"I'm sorry, Mabel. I'm losing my grip. It's unforgivable. William would never understand. It's not the done thing. His family have always maintained their hold."

"Men expect too much of us," I retorted. "They never listen to what we say, except when it suits them."

"William is a good provider. He just expects me to do my job. It is not unreasonable. I can't blame William for my own feelings."

"Isn't he upset about the baby?"

"Of course. Though he doesn't show it much."

"How English."

"But he is, so am I."

"That's the trouble, Mary. I thank God for being part Irish, on my mother's side. I can talk about feelings with her."

"Mine was very beautiful, but we hardly saw her. She was either in bed or entertaining. The servants ran the house, although she was in control, from afar. They would all defer to her. My father doted on her. She could do no wrong. It's a hard act to follow. William expects me to be like her. But I can't."

Mary burst into tears and fell into my arms. She felt so thin and bony. She must have lost a lot of weight. Later, I only managed to sleep fitfully, because I kept worrying about her.

11th July.

Very warm day. I took a stroll to Kensington Gardens. Mary seemed calmer today. She played with the children for most of the morning.

Visited home in the afternoon. Had a splendid time. Mother is looking well. She has missed me, but is now beginning to come out of herself. It is almost a year since father died. Although it was a relief that his long illness was over, it still seems strange not to hear his booming voice echo round the house. Mother has taken up watercolours again, the first time since her marriage. She has begun with some tasteful views of the local park. She says she is going to attempt to do Crystal Palace next. She has stirred me into action. I have taken my box of paints, which I had left at home, and will endeavour to emulate her soon.

13th July.

Dull and cloudy. I slept rather later than usual. There was panic in the household when I came down for breakfast. Mary had not been seen since last night. She had not slept in her bed. William was unavailable in the country. The children seemed unconcerned, they were not told about her disappearance. I felt somehow responsible. Perhaps I should have taken the situation more seriously.

Mary finally returned in the evening, looking surprisingly well. Panic over, but the message to William had already been sent. I eventually spoke to her for a few moments. I think she was trying to avoid me.

"I just had to escape," she explained.

"I thought you were feeling a little better."

"I don't know what to feel any more. It's as if I were dead inside."

"I suppose it's the shock."

"I suppose so."

"Where did you go?"

"Oh, I wondered down by the river. It's a very soothing place. I had a few funny looks," she added, laughing for the first time in weeks.

"You weren't thinking of, er, you know ...?"

She did not reply, and so I assumed that suicide had passed through her mind. Poor Mary. What will become of her? She certainly seems worse since returning from France. I suppose she has been reminded of her terrible loss.

14th July.

Big scene with William, who was annoyed at being called down to London to sort out Mary's "silliness." He stayed only a few hours, saw that she was fit, and then left. She was very apologetic to him and obviously guilty about causing trouble. I do not know whether to pity her or feel angry with her for being so compliant. Is there any real love in their marriage? Or is this what love in marriage is like? Maybe he just blames her for what happened to the baby. Typical. Must be the woman's fault.

15th July.

Did some sketching and watercolours in Kensington Gardens. Very relaxing. Mary was friendly. When we talked, she would not have anything said against William. She defends him to the hilt, and takes all the blame on herself. Unfair.

On the surface, life now seems normal, although I have noticed a certain hesitancy in Mary's attitude to the children. She turns a little away from them when they want a kiss or cuddle. She has always wanted to bring them up herself, as far as possible. She disliked using servants. But now I think that she is relieved to hand them over. She is becoming a stranger. Perhaps I took her friendship for granted. we used to share our innermost thoughts. But since the death of the little boy that has not been possible. I feel bereft of her friendship. It is a real loss for me, too.

19th July.

We started out for the river. It looked a bit cloudy, but not too threatening. Mary was keen to go. Cook prepared a large hamper for us.

I am trying to feel less frustrated with Mary for deserting me. She is the one who needs help and sympathy. I was thinking only of myself. Father would be angry with me. I do miss him. The gruff old thing.

The trip began pleasantly enough. The children were all excited. The coachman drove us down to Molesey and the nanny also came along. She is a strict old bird, but her heart is in the right place, and the children adore her.

When we found a place to stop by the river, the children ran off, leaving Mary and me alone for a while. We sat in silence for a long time.

"I wish I were a child again," she said, suddenly breaking the silence. "I feel like one."

"I wish I could help you more," I said.

"I've been neglecting you. I'm sorry. But I have lost all sense of who I am. I thought I knew. I thought my life was all mapped out. Now I doubt everything."

"You'll get over it."

After another silence, she continued, in a darker mood. "I keep seeing its little eyes, trying to focus on me, searching and not finding. I hate the thing," she said with sudden vehemence. "It won't let me alone. It's still waiting to be fed. I hear it scream-ing with hunger. It's always hungry, and I can't satisfy it. I never have any rest from it."

"You need a doctor," I said with alarm.

"I have tried, but it's no help. He recommended my holiday, which did help for a while. But as soon as we returned, the screams began again. I can't tell William. He'd never forgive me for being so weak and foolish. We've never been that intimate, anyway. Actually, I didn't want the baby."

"You were glad that it died?"

"Yes," she said, with hesitation. "It was a relief not to have to look after another one. It's certainly having its revenge now. There's no rest at night, for, even if I do manage to sleep, it's still there, only ten times bigger and hungrier. I tried running away from home the other night, in the hope that I might escape, but to no avail. He will not let me alone. His eyes keep accusing me of negligence for letting him die."

"But it happens to many mothers. You have been lucky until now."

"That doesn't make it any easier when it happens to you. I myself survived while my baby twin brother died at birth. Apparently, my mother would not look at me for days. Luckily there was a good wet nurse. Maybe that is why my mother and I have never felt that close."

"My mother wanted more children, but she was ill with me and that stopped her from having more. She and I are very close, especially since father died. She needs me more. It feels rather strange—it used to be the other way round."

Before we could talk any further, it began to rain heavily. We quickly rounded up the children and made for some shelter. The rain did not let up, so we consumed our ample and delicious hamper and then returned home by train.

30th July.

We arrived in the morning at Haycroft, Mary's country residence, with its splendid grounds. Must do some painting soon. Had tea at the Drummond Arms. Saw a charming old cottage with an elderly lady in simple dress. Must paint her.

31st July.

Showery but then cleared. I went for a row on the lake. It was very peaceful. Played hide and seek after tea. Then went over garden with Mary. She seemed strangely out of breath during our stroll. She is usually fit and likes a vigorous walk. Possibly a chill coming. The weather has not been very good.

William is somewhere on the estate, rarely seen. Is he avoiding Mary? He does not display much feeling, except for anger and impatience, although he can be playful with the children.

The garden is very impressive. Massive lawns, the romantic lake, the park, and even a maze. Must try the latter some time, but not on my own.

1st August.

Mary awoke in the early hours fighting for breath. The doctor was summoned, but apparently is puzzled by her condition. The cause is not obvious. By late morning, she had recovered, but still felt weak. When I went to her room, she looked frightful—pale and ill.

"It tried to kill me," she said, looking me straight in the eye, as if to measure my reaction. "Do you think I am going mad?"

I did not know what to reply.

"I can see that you think I am," she said, reading my thoughts.

"I don't know what to think, Mary. What did the doctor say?"

"Oh, I did not tell him the truth. He can deal with chills and joint pains, but is hopeless for anything else. William swears by him," she added, with a scornful laugh. This was the first time I had ever heard Mary reveal critical thoughts about William.

"What did you mean, er, just now?" I asked, somewhat anxiously.

"You know, the baby. I could not breathe. It wanted me to join it. It's alone and desperate. Still hungry and pining for me. I thought it had died. You know, Mabel, I must tell you some-thing important ... I no longer believe in God. I lost my faith a long time ago, but I have told no one. I go through the motions for the sake of the children. But I believe that there is such a thing as the Devil. Oh, yes. The mistake that people have made was to think that you had to have God and the Devil. But there is only the one."

"Do you actually believe this?" I asked with some horror.

"As much or as little as anything I believe in."

"How can one live, believing that? I said, not very tactfully.

"Exactly," she replied knowingly. "You cannot. If it weren't for my little ones ..."

I felt near to sobbing with dismay. My friend had changed from the contented mother and friend I had once known. She had been taken over by some malevolent force. She is barely holding on to life. I feel a terrible responsibility. What am I to do? Should I tell William? He at least might take some kind of action, which would perhaps snap her out of her state. But she is insistent that he should remain ignorant.

The more I question her, the more she reveals of the strange logic of her feelings. I would prefer not to know about them, but I am now too involved to retreat. I am afraid that she has already begun to be suspicious of me. I noticed her giving me strange looks, as if she thought I was out to harm her.

2nd August.

We go to church. Driven there. Walked back. Family outing with William. They took pride of place in church. The sermon was really quite interesting, about forgiveness. I observed Mary care-fully but she retained a mask-like expression. Presumably, the service meant nothing to her. I had naively thought she might derive some comfort from it. William was attentive to her and the children. I do not know how much was for show, but I must not malign him. He is not a bad man.

I later suggested to Mary that she join me in some sketching. She used to be quite keen. To my surprise, she agreed. We visited the farm and gardens before settling down near the lake. She took some time to get started, but she soon became absorbed. After a while, she stopped and turned to me.

"It is so long since I took out my paints. I am grateful to you for persuading me to come out here. Drawing helps you see many things more clearly. I have been lost in a confusion of emotions."

"Do you mind me asking you something difficult?" I suddenly found myself saying. As soon as I had spoken, I regretted my words.

"Oh, go ahead, Mabel. I have become quite unshockable."

"Well, what did happen to your baby? You never told me."

"It was only a few days old. It could hardly suck. They wanted to take it from me and give it to a wet nurse. I suppose William is still angry that I refused to allow it. One morning, I awoke and it was dead. Just stopped breathing."

"I'm so sorry. What was wrong with it?"

"Weak from birth, I suppose. The runt," she added with an icy hatred, which frightened me and brought the conversation to an abrupt end.

8th August.

Arrived in London. Mother has a slight illness, but not serious. Will stay until she is better.

11th August.

Had a letter from Mary:

My dear Mabel,

I hope your mother is making a good recovery. I miss your calm presence. I hope that you do not think I have taken you for granted. I have been so preoccupied with myself that I have paid you insufficient attention.

I wanted to tell you the whole truth about the baby, but I did not have the courage to tell you to your face. But it is easier to tell you in writing. It is as if it someone else is speaking for me.

Also, I thought I had better tell you while I am more rational. I had a bad day yesterday. I wandered around the gardens on my own, thinking of the two of us, how we chat and sketch together, when I had an alarming experience. I saw *it* quite clearly, lying on the grass, its tiny fat arms twitching around, its little body shuddering with screams. It was real this time, not a fancy of my dreams or waking thoughts. I then knew that I had to tell the truth to someone, come what may.

When you asked me what happened, I left out the essential fact that I had suffocated the baby. It did not take long. The cries stopped, but of course they have not gone away. I do not know what will become of me now. You must think that I am an evil woman. I did not feel right during the pregnancy. For the first time, I resented having a living thing inside my body, taking the life out of me. Also, the joy of my marriage had gone. William does his duty and expects the same of me. But love has gone. I could not bear to suckle the child under these circumstances. At least the others have known some love, however little and inadequate. The baby I should have loved and cared for seemed merely a thing to hate. I tried to keep these feelings under control, but it knew. In its own unformed way, it knew that I did not love it. That was why it had such a struggle to take food.

Now you know the whole truth. I dare say that you will not want to see me again. I suppose that I must pluck up courage to confess all to William. He will not want a scandal, and so I am sure he will keep the secret. Only life may well become even more unbearable. Perhaps he will forgive me in time. If I do not speak to him, there will always be a terrible barrier between us, which will grow and grow, until we only share hate, and he will not know why. Is that worse than facing him with the truth, so that he will hate me anyway?

I must decide what to do soon. I am being punished for holding on to my secret as much as for killing my little one. It was all mine, and I threw its life away. I do not deserve to live. But then I have others to think of. What would they think of me, if they ever found out? Am I going to be any good to them now? Maybe they would be better off without me. Who knows what I might do to them in the future?

Forgive me for burdening you with my worries, particularly at a time when you are preoccupied with your mother's illness. I do hope that she recovers soon and that you can return here. The children miss you as much as I do.

Yours with affection,
Mary.

What can I add to this moving letter? I had felt that my dear
Mary was withholding something. I should have guessed the
truth. What will she do now? I would like to go to her now, but
I cannot leave Mamma, even though she is on the mend. I will
not sleep tonight. Mary's letter is so shocking. What can be done
for her? Maybe she is right about William keeping the secret.
The last thing that he will want is to have his wife hanged for
murder. She is not under any suspicion. Indeed, it would not
surprise me if her confession were to be dismissed as a result of
illness, a sort of delirium. The last month has indeed felt like
being in the middle of a long, bad dream.

13th August.

Letter from William:

Dear Miss Hope,

I am afraid that I have to inform you of some terrible news. I am
writing to you myself as I know that you were a good friend to
Mary, and that she very much valued your friendship. My dear
wife was killed yesterday afternoon, after falling off her horse.
It had apparently gone out of control, though it had until then
been quite docile. The horse has been put down. I need hardly
say what a terrible shock it has been to us all. Mary was such a
good wife and mother. I and the children will miss her more
than words can express. The funeral will be on Monday 17th
August at 2 pm, at our local church. I very much hope that you
can attend.

Yours sincerely,
Lord William Y.

She did not tell him. I must destroy my diary.

Journal

Such tragic events as described in this story were no doubt more
common than were recognised at the time. Indeed, even now infan-
ticide probably goes unrecognised at times. We still have our secrets
and taboos. I suppose that at least we now understand more about

post-natal depression. Mary became unable to distinguish the real baby from her own mad fantasies about it. The baby became the source of all her bad feelings, and ultimately her persecutor.

Typically in these situations, the husband viewed the problems as emanating from his wife, and offered little substantial support. If he had been more in touch with her, maybe then she would have confided in him. Instead, she had to hide the truth, with disastrous consequences, and the truth died with her. Of course, one wonders whether the horse bolted out of character, or whether Mary herself precipitated her death.

Mary's depression may have been a reaction, in part, to her rather loveless marriage, or perhaps a reflection of her social position—she had all the privileges of her class, but still no effective voice of her own; she remained subservient to her husband.

In some ways, the situation of women, with their special vulnerability in childbirth, has not changed since that time. However, what has changed is the expectation that they are particularly vulnerable in other ways.

I have reached a difficult moment in this writing business, the point when I am not sure how much more I should reveal about my personal life. What began as a diversion from my personal troubles has become an end in itself. When I began, I had little thought of publication, but now that I am approaching what I think will be the end of this collection there may be the chance—or should I say the risk—of publication. Should I then disguise my personal details, as I have done with my patients? Should I retain my anonymity, or have the courage to come clean? It feels easier to divulge details of my individual history than to tackle my marriage. I feel guilty about indirectly using Kathy for the last story. But that, I am afraid, is a result of the ruthlessness of the writing impulse, which weaves everything into its all-embracing mangle.

She knows that I am doing some writing, but I have kept the details from her. I do not think she could face hearing about what I am doing, because she is too vulnerable. Also, I am afraid of what she might say.

I have to keep going. No doubt I am cruel and heartless, a survivor. Has my cruel streak contributed to Kathy's trouble? If I had been a better man, would she have been more able to confide in me? Am I, then, no better than Mary's husband in the story?

Kathy and I are speaking more to one another, and to my great relief she is thinking of going back into therapy. I cannot be her analyst. However, I have also wondered with her whether we should have some marital help. She is not keen on this at the moment, since she feels that she has to sort out her own stuff first. I suppose I feel some relief about this. It sort of absolves me from feeling too responsible for what has been going on. Yet I am also uneasy about this situation. I still wonder how much her wish to keep things to herself is a symptom of our marriage difficulties.

My next story concerns a difficult marital situation, based on that of a professional man I once treated. I have made him into a doctor, a General Practitioner. He obviously also bears some resemblance to me. My writing and my life seem to be merging ...

The country practice

I once knew a country doctor who found himself making a delicate choice about his personal life. I shall begin with a dream he had one Saturday morning in summer.

The doctor felt in the dream that his head was divided into two parts by a kind of ridge. The back part was covered with neatly combed, dark hair and looked healthy and vibrant, like newly laid turf that has been generously watered and has taken root. The hair in the front part, however, was thin and dry. His face in the dream expressed pain and grief, revealing many dense furrows, criss-crossing like parched and cracked earth. In the distance, someone was holding a large knife with a guillotine-shaped blade. The blade leaped out of its handle and hovered over the doctor's head, where the two parts joined. Suddenly, it took off into the sky, came down at great speed and split his head in two.

He awoke with a start, holding his head as if to keep it from falling apart. Once he was conscious enough to realise that it was intact and that his hair was still thick and healthy, he breathed a sigh of relief. A shaft of bright sunlight pierced through a gap in the bedroom curtains and caught him in the eye. He let out a groan, closed his eyes again and searched with his hands for his wife,

Elaine, but in vain because she was already up. He felt empty and lonely, feelings which had become only too familiar to him lately. But as he gradually woke up, his anguish abated, and he crawled out of bed to face the day.

Doctor Ben Chambers was forty-three, a General Practitioner based in a village in Dorset, and was married with three children—sons of fifteen and ten, and a daughter of twelve. He was a small-ish, energetic man, a neat if unimaginative dresser, and reserved in personal encounters. As a doctor, he had grown used to listening to others and perhaps, as a result, rarely allowed himself a degree of open expression of his own feelings. However, although his inner life was kept rather closed, it was full of doubt and confusion. He obtained some relief by immersing himself in his work but recently he had been having a series of troubling dreams, which were upsetting his precarious equilibrium.

The image of the split head continued to hover over him as he began to dress for his Saturday morning surgery, choosing a light green tweed jacket and brown corduroy trousers. He glanced through the bedroom window, taking in the ample garden. Although only mildly warm, it was a bright early summer's day, the sky was already a deep blue, with only a few threads of thin cloud perched on high. Just as he took a deep breath to clear his head, he saw his wife pinning some washing on the line. In the past, the mere sight of her small black panties and brassiere hanging there would have excited him. But now, instead, he felt a sharp stabbing pain in his head just where the dream knife had cut through, as he recalled that it was months since either of them had felt the desire to make love.

As he brushed his hair rather gingerly, for he still felt that his head was vulnerable and tender, his youngest child, Simon, sailed into the room, fondling a pair of white mice.

"Dad, Geraldine doesn't look well. She won't use the wheel. Dad, can you have a look?"

"I'm not a vet, Simon."

"It's all the same, isn't it?" Simon replied with conviction.

"Let's have a look, then."

Simon put one mouse into a trouser pocket, and offered up the other one to his father's clinical gaze.

"Look, dad," said Simon, giving the mouse a little nudge in the ribs and abdomen, and running his fingers down its little limbs.

"She was all right last night, but when I woke up this morning she was all floppy."

"Well, you know, Simon, mice often get ill."

"But you can cure her, can't you?" he replied confidently.

The father had to admit to himself that he still found his son's touching belief in his omnipotence very gratifying—so unlike the attitude of his other children, who had become quite sceptical of his accomplishments and capacities.

"Well, I'll bring home some antibiotics from the surgery. I think Geraldine has a chest infection."

"Will you listen to her with your stethoscope, dad?"

"Of course, Simon."

"Can I listen, too?"

"Of course."

Chambers had been having a number of awkward and wayward thoughts recently, which involved escaping from his family. He now felt guilt spread over him in uncomfortable waves as his son bounced out of the room, with the ailing mouse cuddled lovingly in his hands.

As Chambers made his way down to breakfast, he tried hard to dismiss any awkward feelings from his mind by thinking of medical matters. He was a partner in a two-man practice that was soon to amalgamate with three others in a purpose-built medical centre. This development followed the recent retirement of two politically powerful but incompetent practitioners, who had blocked any progress in service provision. They each had run a single practice in the area, and both were off-duty on Thursdays, on which day you could thus not afford to be ill. However, there was now a group of younger and competent doctors who, with local support, had impressively developed the previously meagre health services. This was especially necessary because several small local hospitals had been closed to save money.

Chambers had drifted into general practice after toying with the idea of going into psychiatry, because he had been vaguely interested in personal problems. He married early, soon found himself with a young family, and then decided that general practice was the best and quickest way to achieve financial security. His wife, Elaine, had been a ward sister at his teaching hospital. She was slim and elegant, with clear blue eyes that had immediately bewitched him. He had found her beautiful and mysterious, a statuesque goddess. She came from a rather unstable family—one brother was schizophrenic, and her parents had separated when she was young. Her father, a surgeon, had run off with one of his trainees, leaving the children with her lawyer mother. Both parents were intelligent but volatile, often at each other's throats, with little regard for their childrens' feelings. But Elaine seemed to Chambers an ideal choice—she was educated, very presentable, keen on having his children, and sensual.

During the first months of their relationship they spent every free moment making love, sometimes risking discovery. For example, they twice made love in the nurse's home, once in the corridor. They managed it in a box with a restricted view at an opera, and once at night in a train station waiting-room, when she sat on him. She particularly thrived on the element of risk—later in their married life, she would even pretend, during love-making, that they were on the verge of being discovered.

As the years passed, he became increasingly aware that there was something lacking in their relationship, despite the arrival of the children and the outward appearance of normality. He could not define precisely what was lacking, but it was something like genuine mutual understanding. Recently, he had found it increasingly difficult to become sexually aroused by her. He had resorted to using pornography to prepare himself for bed, with only limited success. He felt guilty about his lack of interest, but he was also aware that their sexual relationship had become less important to her. Instead, her Catholicism came increasingly to dominate her life, at times to the exclusion of everything else, or so it appeared to him.

Religion had not been an issue when they had met. She was then a lapsed Catholic, and her parents had followed few of its rituals, although she had received Communion. Her mother had showed more interest in the church than her father, particularly after he deserted the family, but even then her interest had been lukewarm.

Elaine, in contrast, became increasingly involved with the small but active local Catholic community. She began going to church several times a week, helped on various church committees, and even joined a Bible study group. She became more inward-looking and preoccupied, as if trying to work out some difficult puzzle in her inner life. Chambers found it increasingly difficult to know how to respond to her, especially since he was irreligious. His father, who had died from cancer when he was seven, was a chartered surveyor. He vaguely remembered him as a quiet and friendly man, who always had a smile. His mother only went out to work after her husband's death, and made a success of a travel and leather goods shop. She was a shy but resolute person, who overcame her social anxiety only with great effort. Chambers admired her but never felt emotionally close to her. Neither parent had been religious. The only substantial belief they held on to with any conviction was in the future of the Labour Party, which they supported through its many crises. To his discomfort, Chambers, who followed his parents' political sympathies, now lived in the kind of place where people still put out Union Jacks with their Conservative Party posters at general elections and where the local MP, a rich squire, would enter the village to the strains of Land of Hope and Glory.

As Chambers came down to breakfast, he tried to put out of his mind all those tiresome thoughts that had been disturbing his life, and which were undermining his faith in himself and his family. Thoughts about leaving his wife, discussing a separation or divorce, or just talking about their situation were too difficult to bear for long without overwhelming him with despair and nausea. He wished it might be possible to have things out in the open and to talk honestly. But half the problem was due to the fact that this seemed impossible.

After he had made himself some coffee and toast and sat down to read The Guardian, Elaine came through the kitchen door to sort out another mound of clothes for drying.

"You're up, Ben," she said dreamily.

"Hmm," he grunted, through a mouthful of toast.

She busied herself with her chores as he worked his way through the news, occasionally throwing a glance her way. She did not seem to notice him, immersed in her own activity. He felt like saying something to her, he yearned to reach out and touch her. It would not have taken much physical effort to make contact but he shrunk from it, finished the paper and made his way to the surgery.

His receptionist, a hard-working but rather nervy woman in her mid-life, was already there organising the notes for his appointments. The first patients had various minor complaints, with which he quickly dealt. One woman had a marital problem she wished to air, one man was anxious about his daughter's difficult adolescent behaviour, and another woman felt depressed for no apparent reason. Chambers was used to dealing with such presenting problems. His partner was a more traditional doctor, who even wore a white coat, and liked to make medical diagnoses. Chambers often dealt with the emotional problems accompanying or causing medical symptoms, and had a reputation for being a good listener.

The morning was fairly routine until the entrance of a Mrs Jean Saunders, a divorcee, who came complaining of vague feelings of fatigue and abdominal discomfort, following a recent mild viral illness. She was a petite woman, in her early thirties, dressed neatly and tastefully. She was a little shy, but appeared warm in spirit and pleasant to know. He found himself becoming deeply interested in her and concerned about her symptoms. He took a detailed history, which did not indicate a major illness, and proceeded to examine her. She removed her tartan dress, green pullover and red blouse, and lay on the examining couch. Chambers had quite often experienced a mild, passing sexual thrill when examining an attractive woman. It was, after all, only to be expected. The important thing was to keep the emotion well under control, and to retain a professional distance.

Although he certainly attempted to follow his usual practice, he found himself experiencing a strong physical attraction towards her. He avoided her eyes, in order to hide his feelings, and proceeded to examine her chest and abdomen, where he found no abnormality.

When she dressed and sat down, looking across his desk at him, grateful for his attention and concerned to hear his views, he became quite flustered. He hid his awkwardness by putting on his very best soothing bedside manner. He explained that he could find nothing wrong, but that he would do some blood tests to be on the safe side. He added that her symptoms were probably the aftermath of the viral illness, and that she would soon recover. He wondered whether a short holiday might help. He was so sympathetic that very soon she found herself talking about how lonely she felt in the village, particularly now that she was divorced. Her ex-husband was an unreliable sort who had embarked unsuccessfully on several hopeless business ventures. The couple had drifted apart, and he had eventually left in order to try his hand abroad. She had not wanted to follow him, since it seemed a good moment to end the relationship. She was an art teacher at the local comprehensive school, where she was reasonably happy. Recently, she had tried to spend more time on her own painting but her fatigue had prevented her from doing very much.

She felt at ease with Chambers, and considerably better after unburdening herself, and better still when he arranged a follow-up appointment a week later.

During the rest of the surgery, he was in a buoyant mood. He was more alert and perceptive than usual, and more decisive in his clinical judgments. But as he set out on a couple of home visits, his mind began to cloud over, and gloom and despondency began to settle over him. It was as if a beautiful illusion had suddenly been swept away by harsh reality. He had no desire to return home for lunch—in fact, he dreaded the prospect. However, his son, Simon, was waiting for the antibiotics for his ailing mouse, and this made Chambers feel guilty about his dread. He thought that he really must be in a bad way if he were obtaining his sexual satisfaction from his patients. He was the one who needed help. He felt it was pathetic, if not dangerous, to behave as he had done.

Yet, he asked himself, what had really happened between him and Jean Saunders? She was merely a lonely, if attractive, woman, who needed to get things off her chest. Yes, but what a chest. That was the problem. He had not dared ask her to remove her black bra in order to listen to her more accurately, for he knew that his hand was trembling at the time. She had such a lovely, full figure and was very feminine. Elaine's body, in contrast, was rather straight and almost masculine. That had never bothered him before, but he now shuddered as he thought of her thin hips and manly bottom.

He tried to shake himself out of his black mood and to put these ridiculous thoughts out of his mind but the more he tried to do so, the more intense were his yearnings for Jean. Then, in a more rational moment, he thought it would be wise to cancel the follow-up appointment with her, or to transfer her to his partner. He had sensed that Jean had also been excited by the encounter and, for that reason, it would be professionally dangerous to continue to see her—he ran the risk of being struck off the medical register if they began a liaison.

He did not know what he wanted from her. He had read about these situations in the medical literature, when, for example, a hysterical patient might entrap a doctor in order to cause trouble, or when an unscrupulous male doctor might take advantage of his patient's vulnerability to gratify his own needs. Was he himself some kind of abusing monster?

Perhaps he was imagining everything. Maybe there had been no mutual attraction, no seduction, and no real danger, except in his fantasy. It was all a misunderstanding. He had started the day with a bad dream, which had clouded his judgment. He reasoned that it would be better to retain the next appointment with Jean, if only to eliminate all these disturbing thoughts once and for all.

For the rest of that day, Chambers was subdued. The encounter in the surgery had frightened him. He realised how susceptible he now was to an affair. His home could no longer provide him with security. He was also sexually frustrated after six months of celibacy. The few times that Elaine and he had tried to talk about the situation, she had shrugged her shoulders as if it say she was helpless to do anything about it. After a while, it had become a habit for them to go to bed at separate times, so that one would be asleep before the other.

The following morning, he awoke feeling surprisingly refreshed and cheerful. He jumped out of bed with unusual alacrity and strode down to breakfast before the others. Later, he mowed the lawn, which he had been neglecting for some time. The physical exertion and the pleasure from transforming the untidy mess of long grass into a neat lawn again produced an intense feeling of sexual desire for the first time in months. Until then, his sexuality had been sort of hibernating, because it had no satisfactory outlet. He allowed himself to fantasise about Jean Saunders. He imagined her body stretched across his examining couch, naked and receptive. He banished any guilty feelings, persuading himself that his fantasies were incapable of being realised.

Because he had worked up a thirst, he decided to have a drink at the pub across the road from the house. It was nearly lunchtime and the bar was filling. There were a few retired people, a farmer, some bikers and, sitting alone in a corner, Jean Saunders, who was sipping a gin and tonic. Of course, since they both lived in the village, he had seen her before she had come to the surgery, but only at a distance.

Now she gave him a warm smile, which he returned. He could hardly ignore her just because she was his patient—after all, most of the people in the pub were also his patients and he was on cordial terms with them, as was to be expected in a country practice.

As he sat with his beer at the bar, Jean came up beside him, with her glass held out to the publican.

"I'll get you this one," Chambers said.

"That's very kind of you."

"How are you?"

"Very well, now," she replied, with a meaningful smile.

"Ah, good, good," he said, slightly flustered. "I, er, I'm glad," he continued, his ears burning like a schoolboy's. He took a couple of gulps of beer to calm himself and then, to his surprise, he coolly suggested that they go over to her table. Once they were settled, she said, casually and with a seductive smile, that she was looking forward to their next meeting.

"Are you?" he replied, equally casually.

"I feel as if a burden has been lifted."

"You're exaggerating, Mrs Saunders."

"Jean, please, Dr Chambers."

"Jean. And, er, I'm Ben."

"Ben," she said, savouring the name. "A nice name. Solid."

"Oh, that's me all right," he said, with a self-deprecating laugh.

"But I can see there's more to you," she added.

"I'm sure I don't know what."

"Perhaps I shouldn't say," she said coyly.

"Why not?"

She hesitated, but then said in a whisper: "Passion. Oh, yes."

For a while, he pretended not to have heard what she had said. He let his eyes wander around the room, feigning curiosity about what was going on there. Then he glanced back at her. No, she had not disappeared. She was not a phantom of his imagination. Finally, he said: "I don't think you should see me at the surgery again, Jean."

"Oh," she said with disappointment.

"What I mean is … You know … Let's meet somewhere else."

"Yes, of course," she replied, reassured.

Their next meeting took place one afternoon when he was supposedly doing some home visits. He drove her to a secluded wood, where they talked and embraced. Unlike Elaine, she was easy to talk to and calmly reassuring. When, a couple of weeks later, they made love at her house, he found her receptive and responsive. While he thought that their affair might be too good to be true, he also felt that he deserved some pleasure and fun after his months of angst.

During the first weeks of their relationship, Chambers was in an almost permanent state of well-being, and was attentive to Elaine. However, after the excitement of his secret encounters began to wane a little, he began to have doubts about his behaviour. He asked himself what would happen if Jean wanted more than an affair. Would she tell Elaine? Suppose the affair were to end bitterly, would Jean then tell the medical authorities? These doubts and fears interfered with the progress of the affair, until both parties finally shared their concerns. Jean felt guilty about what they were doing. She was very much aware of the risks to his professional standing, but she had changed doctors at once. Furthermore, she reasoned that they lived in a small community, where such situations did occur on occasion. Everyone knew each other's business—indeed, their relationship was probably already common knowledge. But at the same time, the villagers knew when to close ranks. Besides, she added, didn't he know that his wife was unpopular in the village? He confessed that this was news to him. She explained that it was partly the result of prejudice about her Catholicism, but it was mainly because of her superior attitude. Her nickname was "Lady Muck." No one would complain if she were brought down a peg or two.

He was shocked by these revelations and by his own ignorance of Elaine's reputation. Even when he had betrayed her, he had held her in high esteem. He felt as if a part of himself had been attacked. After all, they had been married for some fifteen years, ten of them in the village. He had loved her for that time, and perhaps still did. Yet why had he been so blind to her faults? He had fallen for her elegance and mystery. He had put her on a pedestal, but now he began to see through the illusion he had created. Without that illusion, he even doubted if there was anything substantial in their relationship. Perhaps Elaine had lost her belief in him, and for that reason had turned to religion for comfort.

His disillusionment with Elaine completed a process of detachment from her, though he was very concerned about the childrens' welfare were they to divorce. He had recently been more responsible for their care since Elaine had spent increasingly more time at her religious meetings. She had become involved in a religious community which offered some kind of help for its members, as well as placements for vulnerable adults such as ex-psychiatric patients. His youngest child, Simon, in particular, was becoming increasingly troubled by his mother's absences and the obvious marital trouble. He kept asking his father penetrating questions about his parents, which Chambers found extremely difficult to answer.

The situation soon reached a point when Chambers felt an overwhelming need to confront Elaine with the truth. But it was difficult finding time to talk, for they both had busy schedules and had also become adept at avoiding one another. But, eventually, one evening, when the children were finally out of the way, he said to her that he needed to have a serious talk. They sat face to face in the lounge.

"Being so serious doesn't suit you, Ben dear," said Elaine mockingly.

In the past, he would have welcomed her remarks as part of their mutual banter, but now he found it merely irritating.

"Yes, well …" he began, trying to curb his annoyance. "Look, Elaine …" He paused for a moment, trying to find the appropriate words to express the complexities of their unhappy situation.

"Yes, Ben?"

"Look, we do need to talk."

"Do we?"

"*I* do, at least."

"What is there to talk about?"

"You know very well. It's about us."

"I have nothing to say," she said dismissively.

"But we can't go on like this."

She became flustered and confused, and refused to look him in the face. "I'm sure … I'm not really … Can't go on, you say?"

"We must talk, Elaine."

"You just said that."

"It's not right between us any more. You must know that."

She looked at him blankly and then refused to converse. He felt that a terrible chasm had just opened up between them, and that if either were to make one step towards the other, they would fall into that chasm and be lost. He shuddered as he sensed her inner fear and experienced her terrible silence. But he also thought that he ought at least to tell her the truth about Jean, and that it was a serious relationship. All this was received in dumb silence. He felt as if he were violating her with his words, and that each sentence was a body blow, but the urge to come clean took him over.

The situation quickly resolved itself soon after this encounter took place. Elaine kept to herself for several days, refusing to speak to him, and also avoiding the children. Then she left the family home and took up residence in the religious community. Chambers had the main care of the children, who dealt with the separation reasonably well, although with some counselling. They had intermittent contact with their mother, but she seemed more concerned about herself, as if she had given up on them.

Eventually, Chambers and the children left the village when he joined another practice. Jean soon joined him, and they eventually married. The last I heard was that she was expecting twins.

Journal

Doctors sleep with their patients more often than is generally recognised—like sexual abuse of children, it is only recently that the truth has begun to come out. It is perhaps debatable about whether or not Chambers abused Jean, even though she was his patient. After all, she was an adult, and there was genuine affection between them. Admittedly, there was also an initial element of tease and seduction, but there is in any love affair. On the other hand, he did rather abuse his position at a time when Jean was vulnerable and grateful to him.

Elaine's world crumbled around her. She really had some kind of breakdown. I think that I have always been attracted to madness. One of my earliest memories, from about the age of three, is that of a mad woman dancing along the street in the afternoon, while I was playing with my friends. The other children laughed at her, but I tried to make them feel sympathy for her. I did not succeed, and she was abusive to all of us. The incident has left its mark on me. I have an ambiguous relationship to madness and to mad women—I am sane, while the mad person is running away from me, and I am left sad and helpless. I was not sure whether or not to follow that woman. Whether or not to remain immobile, or to join her in her frenzied dance. It is no coincidence, then, that my profession involves trying to make sense of people's confusion. I may also be attracted to madness in an unhealthy way and may even, in some way I do not understand, precipitate it in others, in Kathy for example. The possibility frightens me.

Another early memory, from when I was seven, comes to mind, when I went out of control on my tricycle. That may sound ridiculous, but I remember being determined from that time on never to have a similar experience if I could possibly help it, and to avoid any situation which might put me at risk of losing control. I had this ridiculous rickety blue tricycle, with thin, hard tyres and a lumpy saddle. God, I was ashamed of it. I wanted a proper bike, but my parents said they were too dangerous. I was happy enough to have something on wheels, so I could join my friends, but before I dared to show them I decided, rather cleverly in retrospect, to try it on my own.

Either I underestimated that machine, or else I secretly determined to write it off so that my parents would get me a proper bike. It certainly had a kick to it—it was seriously dangerous, as if it were under a spell.

I set out near the top of the steepish hill on which we lived. But then I hurtled down that hill, totally out of control. I still do not know how it happened. I eased on to the saddle and pushed off gently, but then it took off like a mad thing. I felt every change of paving stone, every bump and crack on the pavement, every chip and fragment. The bottom of the hill was rushing up at an alarming rate, as if I had fallen off a high building. I tried frantically moving the handlebars and grabbing the brakes, while screaming out in panic. But my frantic attempts to stop the machine only seemed to increase its speed. Then I gave up trying to control it and let it go where it wished. It finally came to a halt just before the pavement led onto a road, by crashing into a tree. The handlebars were all twisted, my knees were badly grazed, but otherwise I was uninjured. I managed to push the bike home, and it was thrown away. Eventually, my parents were persuaded to get me a real bicycle. I still feel a little nervous when I travel at speed and I try to avoid situations which make me feel like I am back on that machine, not knowing where I am being led and whether or not I will stop.

I tried to stop thinking about these stories for a couple of weeks, but this only made me feel miserable. Nor did it help me deal better with the situation at home, which at least has not deteriorated.

My last story in this collection came to mind after reading some Greek tragedy. They often seem to be about the disintegration of a family. Clearly I am worried that this might happen to my own family. It certainly happened to the family of the patient who also inspired the story. She stayed for a long analysis, at the end of which her ghosts were finally laid to rest. Perhaps also a message of comfort for me.

Twist of a knife

Cleo was wondering when her wealthy husband would return home from one of his many business trips abroad. She was in her mid-thirties, tall, elegant, and queenly. She lived in a large mansion in Chelsea with her children, a son and a daughter. She was not impatient for her husband to return. On the contrary, she was dreading it.

There was a time when she could not bear to be parted from him, but that was years before, when she was in her early twenties and newly married. She was then a submissive young woman, very much in love with her charming and witty husband, the youngest son of a large and well-connected upper class family. She had met him while undertaking market research for his finance company, of which he was then a junior executive. She came from a poor Yorkshire family. Her father, a forthright miner, was a harsh disciplinarian, who used physical violence on the children and his wife. Her mother, a rather quiet and passive woman, did little to protect her children from his attacks. Cleo, a bright girl, went to university in York. After graduation, she moved to London to work in the City. She was a lively, attractive, and ambitious girl, who did well there. She set her sights on either making or marrying money.

She had had her fill of privation as a child and was determined never to be poor again.

Cleo's husband, Stephen, was a fairly typical product of the English upper class. He went to boarding school, where he learned to hide his feelings and play the game. He was a popular boy, good at sport, and a natural choice for captain of various teams. Though not particularly academic, he managed to do well enough to enter Oxford to read history, where he obtained an average degree. His family connections enabled him to join a large City firm, where he gradually worked his way up the ladder. He was popular with clients because of his charm and his good business instinct. His success was such that in his mid-thirties, he became a chief executive. It was thus only a short step from being captain of cricket at his public school to being a captain of British industry.

The marriage began well but soon deteriorated, particularly after the birth of their first child, Elizabeth. Stephen found the sight of his pregnant wife quite offensive. He could hardly bear to look at her swollen abdomen. He was glad to have a child, in the abstract, but was unable to give Cleo the help and support she needed as a young, anxious mother. His attitude spoiled for her the pleasure of her pregnancy. Despite herself, she became resentful towards the developing foetus. She had nightmares about it, imagining that it would be born deformed because of her negative thoughts about it. Stephen spent more time out of the house as the pregnancy progressed. Cleo felt more and more lonely and isolated. She joined an ante-natal class, which Stephen would not attend, giving the excuse that he was too busy at work. His disinterested attitude gradually made her feel more resentful towards him, and less tolerant and submissive. By the time that their baby daughter was born, Cleo's attitude had changed dramatically. She became hard and aloof, quarrelsome and unwilling to lose an argument.

Initially, her personality change could have been put down to post-natal depression, for she could hardly bear to look at her new baby. She refused to breast feed, because she disliked the close and intimate feel of mouth on breast. Fortunately for the baby, Cleo's mother came to stay for a while, and looked after it for most of the time, until Cleo forced herself to pay it some attention.

Stephen was pleased with the birth of his daughter, but he left her care to the women. Cleo had little doubt that by now he was having affairs, but she no longer cared about what he did. She became more self-preoccupied, and decided that she needed to build up a more separate life. The arrival of their second child, Alexander, was more pleasurable for Cleo. By then, they had employed an experienced and tender-hearted middle-aged nanny, Theresa, who loved caring for young children. She was only too glad to take he children off Cleo's hands for most of the day.

Stephen's attitude to his son was markedly different from that towards his daughter. Much to Cleo's annoyance, he paid him considerably more attention. Alex came to resemble his father more and more as he grew up. He became a miniature public-school boy, well-behaved and polite, scornful of too much open expression of feeling. Elizabeth was more lively—rather seductive, even when young, and prone to outbursts of temper. But she was also devoted to her brother.

Life for the children was happy enough, thanks to Theresa's devotion to them, but the family was divided. There were deep and seemingly unresolvable divisions between husband and wife. On the surface, they were an ideal couple—lavish entertainers, amusing dinner guests, and devoted parents. Furthermore, they had style. Cleo had a good eye, and enjoyed spending pots of money on decorating and adorning their large house. Her desire to have the good things in life was never satiated. Stephen was a good provider and she was a good spender. But not far below the surface, they were dissatisfied with one another. He did not give her the time and attention she craved, while she seemed incapable of satisfying his need for a woman who would both tolerate his boyishness and excite his sexual desire. They continued to sleep with one another, but infrequently.

His affairs were not a matter for discussion. In time, she even felt that they were convenient for her, as it enabled her to have a degree of independence from him that she otherwise might not have had. But she was also deeply hurt by him. She felt that he despised her for coming from the working class, although she had managed to disguise her origins very convincingly.

Over the years, she managed to create for herself a powerful new persona. She became an imposing matriarch and business aid. She became important for his career, managing the social side of his financial deals with consummate skill.

One year, when the children were well into adolescence, Stephen had to spend a lot of time in New York in order to set up a new business. Cleo then finally took a lover, another businessman, a few years her junior. Victor was a banker, born in Canada but brought up by his English mother in London, after his parents had divorced when he was a child. He remained devoted to his mother, a kindly lady who suffered from occasional "nervous" fits, when she would take to her bed and remain mute for two or three days.

Victor was overweight, with a large paunch and a double, or treble, chin, and he sweated a lot. Though hardly attractive in appearance, he was easy company, did not make too many emotional demands and had a good sense of humour. He was a good companion for Cleo—he made her feel wanted again. She managed to keep their affair secret for some time, except from her mother, whom she saw from time to time. The old lady sympathised with her daughter's wish for more recognition. She herself had not had a happy marriage. Her husband had been insensitive and domineering. He had even beaten up on several occasions. Although Stephen was not physically violent, he had always treated Cleo with a certain amount of contempt.

Stephen had to remain in New York for longer than originally anticipated, although he managed to make a couple of brief visits home. Their period of separation gave Cleo time to reflect upon her life and marriage, both of which had become, for her, sterile. Her children would soon be leaving home, and her husband was no longer interested in maintaining a full relationship. She had given up her work and had not replaced it with anything worthwhile. She had put her husband and children before her own needs and desires, and now she feared a lonely old age. She also felt that it would not be long before Stephen would finally ditch her. He would probably find some young thing who would excite him and pander to him more effectively than she could. On the other hand, the prospect of doing without her current material comforts alarmed her. She reasoned that she would have to find a way of securing the comfortable life to which she had become accustomed. Victor provided a solution, in that he was also wealthy.

She decided to throw down the gauntlet. She asked Victor to live with her. Not surprisingly, he was rather shocked by her proposal, because she and Stephen were not separated. However, Victor had become very attached to her. They saw each other most days, and he had come to rely on her. She was the first woman, apart from his mother, to whom he had become deeply attached. When he expressed reluctance about moving in with her, Cleo hinted that she would end with him if he did not agree to her request. He agreed to being introduced to the children and to spending weekends with them, but he refused to live there full-time, using the excuse that his sickly mother still needed him. Cleo temporarily accepted the compromise.

The children were stunned by Victor's arrival on the scene. They knew that their parents' marriage was unsatisfactory—Cleo had never made a secret of her feelings on the matter. They even knew of, and were accustomed to, their father's affairs. But they naively thought that their mother would never do the same, and they were angry with her, especially since Victor was, in their eyes, such a slob.

However, Cleo ignored both their distress and their resentment. She was set on bringing Victor into the home, partly to spite Stephen, partly to test out his reaction, and partly because she was lonely and in need of love. She was bitter about having becoming bitter with life. She had thrown herself into her marriage, full of hope and expectations. Then she had become an all-too experienced woman of the world, who had learned to live with chronic betrayal for the sake of a few drops of affection. She wanted her revenge.

By the time that Stephen was due to return, Victor had moved in for most of the week, Stephen's clothes were put in a spare room, and the children kept to themselves in their own part of the house. They had thought of letting their father know about the situation, but in the end they decided not to because, although they tended to side with him against their mother, they also resented his absence. They decided to lead virtually separate lives from both parents, with the result that they both grew up rapidly and were precocious in their attitudes and behaviour. The house became a focus for young people, particularly those with delinquent leanings. Cleo let the children do their own thing, provided that they did not encroach upon her life.

The arrangement worked reasonably well, until the time for Stephen's arrival drew near, when tension began to mount. Victor's first impulse was to beat a hasty retreat. He disliked angry scenes and dreaded the consequences of Stephen finding out what had happened in his absence. Victor felt most uncomfortable about being a usurper. On the other hand, he adored Cleo and would do virtually anything for her.

The big confrontation between Cleo and Stephen never occurred, because instead of returning from New York, he sent the following telegram: DECIDED TO LIVE HERE. SURE YOU WON'T MIND. KEEP THE HOUSE. SORT OUT REST LATER. LOVE KIDS. STEPHEN.

After the initial shock, Cleo was furious with him. She tried to contact him, but only obtained his answering machine at home and a stubborn secretary at work, who insisted that he was unavailable. Eventually, she sent her own telegram demanding his return. The next message she received was from his lawyer, offering a lump sum payment and generous maintenance if she agreed to a legal separation. She discovered that he was living with a wealthy New York socialite. All Cleo's plans for revenge on him appeared to have been thwarted. Unable to tackle him in person, she took out her rage on his clothes and possessions. She burnt the suits, shirts, and other articles one by one on a large bonfire, assisted by Victor and observed from afar by the children from their bedrooms. She retained any valuable objects and gave the rest to Oxfam. Her anger knew no bounds for a few weeks. She fired off several vicious telegrams, bombarded his home and work with insulting messages, vowed to tear him limb from limb, but could not summon the desire to go to the States to confront him directly.

It was not the fact that he had deserted her which annoyed her so much as the fact that he had pre-empted her rejection of him. She informed him of Victor's presence in the house, in the hope that he might return home to do the decent thing and kick him out, but Stephen left all communications with her to his lawyer, and remained in New York.

As her acute anger died down, Cleo turned to Victor for help. He was both surprised and flattered by her new attitude towards him. Until then, he had felt himself to be a mere appendage to her, but after the crisis he came to have increasing importance in her life. The children, however, were resentful of Victor, particularly as he became more confident about his position in the house. They refused on principle to comply with any request made by him, however small. Cleo was unable to change their attitude—indeed, they came to hate her as she turned her attention to him.

The childrens' feelings of isolation and abandonment were increased by the fact that Stephen appeared to give them little thought, only occasionally making contact with them. His new woman was expecting a baby, and she and his work seemed to be of primary importance to him.

Elizabeth had by then become a pretty girl, nearly sixteen, with long, straight black hair, a trim figure, and a taste for brightly coloured clothes. She attracted boys and revelled in their attentions, although she had no particular boyfriend. Victor, who had at first avoided encountering the children as much as possible, could not ignore Elizabeth's budding sexuality. He tried to talk to her with a sort of fatherly concern, which did not come naturally to him and which repelled her. He tried various means to be in her company, for example escorting a friend who had called up to her room, or by offering to bring her breakfast in bed. To cover his true motivation, he also offered to bring Alexander breakfast. Although Elizabeth was not fooled by Victor's obvious behaviour, she decided to string him along in order to spite her mother for bringing him into the house. She allowed him to carry the tray of croissants, coffee, and orange juice to her room and to place it by the side of her bed. Her room was decorated with bright primary colours, the walls were covered with posters of pop stars, and her clothes were strewn all over the floor. Victor enjoyed entering her chaotic adolescent world. After depositing the tray, he would ruffle the bedclothes to wake her up, and sometimes as a joke would make some critical comment about the mess. He particularly enjoyed picking up some small item of clothing, such as a pair of knickers or a skimpy T-shirt, and placing them on the chest of drawers. Sometimes, she would pretend to be fast asleep so that he had to shake her awake. She would then throw off the bedclothes to reveal her skimpy nightdress. Cleo was apparently unaware of these activities. It took her hours to go off to sleep, despite the use of pills and alcohol, and so she slept in late.

The game between Elizabeth and Victor continued for some weeks, increasing Victor's preoccupation with her and her stranglehold over him. It was not long before he was desperate to have sex with her, but he did not dare make the first move. She enjoyed

having some power over him, and felt an additional pleasure knowing that Cleo appeared to be ignorant of what was going on.

However, the atmosphere in the house became increasingly
charged, as if someone had doused the place in petrol, and it was
just waiting for someone to strike a match in order to set it ablaze.
Cleo began to notice Victor's meaningful glances towards Elizabeth
at the table, although Elizabeth remained indifferent to him.
Alexander was a party to his sister's tactics, and found them mildly
amusing. He was also quite fond of Victor, because he missed his
father and at least Victor provided some sort of masculine presence
in the house. Elizabeth despised her father for abandoning them—
she also held her mother responsible for the marriage breakdown.
She had not forgotten that Cleo had brought Victor into the house
before Stephen had formally decided to remain in New York.
Alexander, who was more forgiving, determined in secret to try to
join his father when he left school.

After a while, Elizabeth decided to heat up her relations with
Victor. She led him to believe that, if he came home early when her
mother was not in the house, she would provide him with special
favours. When Cleo spent the day in town with a friend, Victor
sneaked back after lunch, while Elizabeth took the day off school.

When he arrived, he heard the pulsating sounds of pop music
coming from Elizabeth's room. He trembled with anxious excitement as he anticipated what he might find there. He felt like an
explorer about to stumble on the source of a powerful river after
negotiating his way through hundreds of miles of thick jungle. He
crept slowly towards her room. For a second, the thought crossed
his mind that this was his last chance to turn back, but he could not
stop his hand from tapping at the door, or his voice from calling out
to her as sweetly as he could manage, "It's me, Victor."

The door opened. "Hello, Victor," she said, with a wicked little
smile.

"Er, hello," he replied nervously. His legs took him further into
the room.

"What's the music?" he asked, staring at her body as if mes-
merised. She was wearing a long, flowing, purple silk dressing
gown, which was hanging loosely so that he had glimpses of her
pert breasts, a flash of tummy, and an impression of lacy black
knickers.

"Let's dance, Victor," she said, firmly taking him by the arms.

He could feel her breath on his neck. At last he was close to her. She had always refused to kiss him or be kissed by him. Finally, he had his chance to be intimate with her. He had some doubts about the wisdom of what he was doing, but he continued to dance with her. He put a hand on her bottom and gave it a little squeeze. She made a little wiggle, as if finding this pleasurable. But just as he was about to go further, she pushed him away.

"That's enough," she said coldly.

He was dumbfounded. "What do you mean?" he said, like a sulky boy who had been refused a toy.

"It's bye-bye time," she replied, tying the belt of her dressing gown. "I have work to do," she added with a yawn. She went over to her desk and attended to some books and papers, while he stood there not knowing which way to turn.

"But ... I thought ..." he started.

"I don't care what you thought," she interrupted. "Get out of my room, or I'll make a fuss."

He eventually obeyed and made a sheepish exit. She locked her door and collapsed on to her bed with paroxysms of laughter. She had made him look a complete idiot, and she was very pleased with herself. Victor crept out of the house and returned to his office, where he tried to lose himself in routine business.

When he attempted to bring breakfast in bed to Elizabeth the following morning, he found that she had locked the door. She refused to let him in, and told him to leave the tray outside the room. That was the end of his breakfast ministrations.

Soon Victor changed his overt attitude to Elizabeth. He kept his distance, and lost no opportunity to put her down in front of Cleo. When he was alone with Cleo, he constantly denigrated Elizabeth as being lazy and a delinquent. He was very hurt by the trick she had played on him—Elizabeth remained indifferent to him, and ignored his negative comments about her, which only increased his anger and resentment towards her.

Cleo was puzzled by the vehemence of his attacks on Elizabeth. Her first thought was there must be some sinister reason for them, but she decided to say nothing in order to see what might be revealed. She had begun to notice worrying signs of ageing on her face. Her eyes were becoming baggy, her brow had too many wrinkles, and her mouth was too pinched. For the first time, she doubted her capacity to keep Victor. Until then, she had taken him for granted. But she decided to be more attentive to him, however much effort it cost her. She had no desire to be ditched by him, and she still feared a lonely old age.

The children noticed that Victor and Cleo had a new and firmer alliance, that she stopped sniping at him, and even gave him the occasional smile. Elizabeth was alarmed by this turn of events. It was not the result she had hoped for from her actions. To her frustration, it seemed that once again her mother would come out on top. Elizabeth had intended to attack her mother via Victor. She found him physically rather repulsive, but was otherwise not that bothered about him. She just could not bear her mother being happy. Elizabeth could not recall a time when her mother had been openly affectionate to her. There had always been a barrier between them. Cleo had never been able to make up for her early rejection of her daughter when she was a baby, while Elizabeth's adolescence had brought to the surface many of Cleo's fears about ageing and losing her looks. Mother and daughter were locked into a vicious circle of mutual disappointment and rejection.

Elizabeth began to go through a worrying period of introversion. She locked herself in her room for hours on end, refusing even to let in Alexander. When she emerged, she would wander around the house in a dream-like state, barely acknowledging the existence of others. Even Cleo became worried about her, but whenever she tried talking to her she was greeted by a hateful, icy stare. Soon, Elizabeth spent more and more time out of the house, apparently with friends. She would not say where she was going, and refused to say when she would return. Sometimes she came back late at night, and was occasionally out all night. When challenged about her behaviour, she would clam up. She was even indifferent to the threat of cutting off her generous allowance. She looked like a ghost, with a pale, drawn face and dead eyes. Her appearance greatly affected Cleo, who seemed to see in her daughter some kind of avenging angel come to persecute her for all her failings as a mother.

The school also worried about Elizabeth, because she did not concentrate and was very moody. Finally, they detected that she was addicted to heroin, and was in desperate need of help.

Cleo was shocked, but not totally surprised, by the discovery of her daughter's addiction, for clearly something had been amiss with her. She contacted Stephen, who agreed to pay the fees for a private clinic. Elizabeth was quickly shipped off there in order to begin a withdrawal programme. It turned out that she had been associating with a group of wealthy young Sloane Rangers, most of whom were into drugs. She had also been dealing and was lucky to escape prosecution. She still refused to talk to her mother, maintaining an icy distance, even when she returned home drug-free.

Cleo tried hard to be kind to her but, try as she might, she was unconvincing. Elizabeth was not fooled by her mother's strained attempts to show her warmth. Cleo could not feel warm towards her, because Elizabeth's problems constantly reminded her of her failings as a mother. It was like having a mirror held up to her, reflecting back her inadequacies. Perhaps that was why Elizabeth, in turn, reflected back to her mother as little emotion as possible. Certainly, the effect of the addiction had been to deaden her emotions.

The clinic did a reasonably good job, but she remained a difficult young woman, unwilling, or unable, to express herself, and full of anger and self-loathing. She cut her arms with a razor blade on a couple of occasions at the clinic. They were only superficial cuts, but they left faint scars, evidence of her inner turmoil.

Victor continued his campaign against Elizabeth, using her addiction as yet more evidence of her impossible character. Alexander felt cut off from his sister. He felt that she had isolated herself as if she were contaminated by radioactivity.

Elizabeth felt herself an increasing burden as the "sick" member of the family. She felt it was unjust to be singled out as the problem, when she felt that her mother was at least partly to blame for much of what had happened. But she felt powerless to act effectively and unable to confront her mother with her feelings of rage and despair. She found it difficult facing the world without the comfort of drugs. Oblivion had been an attractive state of mind. Drugs were kind friends, always available when needed, and capable of removing the feeling of emptiness. Without them, she felt loneliness and despair. But she tried hard not to associate with her drug-oriented friends. Instead, she tried to turn to schoolwork, and to associate with more normal adolescents. But she still felt different from the others, world-weary and hardened to life.

Just as she was beginning to feel a little more stable, Victor made another sexual advance towards her. It happened one morning, when she came down to breakfast unusually early, after a restless night. Victor was at the table with his coffee and croissant, before going off to the office. They barely acknowledged each other, but he could not fail to notice that she was naked beneath her dressing gown. She made little effort to conceal her body and, as she took mouthfuls of toast and sipped at her coffee, her breasts became visible. She did not appear to notice the effect of this on Victor, because she was preoccupied with night thoughts concerning what she should do with her life and how she was to escape from home. She felt trapped in her mother's house. She was too young to support herself, but she felt that being at home was robbing her of her wish to live.

Victor lingered at the breakfast table, leering at her. She was still immersed in her thoughts, barely aware of his presence. He got up from the table and carried his plate and cup to the dishwasher and, as he started to leave the room, he looked once more at Elizabeth and then stood a few paces behind her. Just as she became aware of his menacing presence, he pushed himself towards her, put both of his large, fat arms around her neck and placed his small hands on her breasts. He smothered her neck with wet kisses.

"You bitch," he hissed through the kisses.

"Leave me alone," she said, as she struggled to free herself from his grip.

"You know you want it," he said, as his hands reached down to her tummy, kneading and caressing her flesh. "Come on, come on," he added with desperate passion.

"Get off!" she screamed, as his large body enveloped her and took her over.

"I want you, I want you," he mumbled, kissing her neck and behind the ears, even though she was struggling, and tried to butt his mouth with her head. Yet he was too strong for her, and she could hardly move.

One of his hands managed to creep down to her crotch. She stopped struggling and let him play with her for a few seconds, to give him the illusion that she was submitting to him. As his grip relaxed, she managed to free one arm and grabbed the bread knife from the table nearby. She quickly slashed at him with it. It cut the side of his neck and he squealed with pain. As he let go of her and instinctively reached for the wound, she turned round and thrust the blade hard into his stomach, twisting the knife in the new wound with all her strength. He fell to the floor, with the knife still stuck in him, and with blood spurting all over the kitchen. She rushed out of the room in a frenzy, went straight to her bedroom and had a shower to rinse off the blood as quickly as possible. Once she had dressed, she began to realise what she had done, and returned to the kitchen. He was laying there, apparently dead. She felt numb. She could not believe what had happened, but managed to call an ambulance. Then she went to her mother's bedroom, woke her up and said to her quietly: "I have killed Victor. He was molesting me."

Then she went to her room to await the consequences of her action.

Victor survived the attack, though only just. Elizabeth was charged with attempted murder but, because of the circumstances of the attack, was found not guilty. By then, Victor had had enough of Cleo and her family, and broke off contact with them. Elizabeth did not return home, but found a place in a hostel for vulnerable young people. Alexander left for America soon afterwards to live with his father. Cleo was left on her own, refused to have anything to do with Elizabeth, and carried on her life as before, with little regard.

Journal

Cleo was adept at passing on suffering to others, particularly her daughter, rather than experience it herself. Elizabeth turned to drugs, rather than her mother, when she needed comfort. The absence of caring and concern began with the parents' marriage. Although for a while it seemed to work on the surface, it soon became plagued with unresolvable divisions which ultimately had near-fatal consequences. No doubt Cleo's violent childhood had left its mark on her, making it difficult to be affectionate.

There are certain similarities between this story and the Greek tragedy of Electra. Victor was the usurper, like Aegistheus. Stephen, the Agamemnon figure, was not actually killed, but remained permanently away from home. Elizabeth had the haunted character of the fatherless and mother-hating Electra. In addition, there is the theme of murderous hatred, which underpinned much of the story. For example, there was, as it were, the murder of mother love and the destruction of the life-link between mother and child—which began with Cleo's post-natal depression, from which she never really recovered.

Although an unruly and difficult adolescent, Elizabeth partly acted that way as a consequence of being the family's scapegoat, the target for all kinds of destructive feelings. Cleo probably blamed her birth for Stephen's desertion from the family. The psychical damage to Elizabeth started from that time, and was repeated when Elizabeth became a sexual rival to her mother at adolescence. Cleo treated her daughter as if she were not a developing person in her own right, but a mirror that reflected back her own inadequacies. Elizabeth's provocation of the misnamed Victor was probably an attempt to deal with her mother's jealousy of her youth.

I have charted the disintegration of a family where hate predominated over love. Although this is not true in my own case, I now doubt the strength of my marriage. I wonder how many more knocks it can take before it finally disintegrates, how long before the bricks and mortar of the family home collapse. I feel rather like a tightrope walker who does not know whether to advance or retreat, but who realises that there is danger below and that he has to keep going one way or else he will fall.

My writing has been very useful in that it has given me an outlet for the expression of my doubts and uncertainties. I have also occasionally simply enjoyed making up stories. But all along I have been concerned about how much the project may have diverted me from facing up to the realities of my situation. Although Kathy and I have begun to face our difficulties, there is a long way to go before we can resolve them. In a sense, we are faced by problems due to subtle changes over the years. My fear is that if we sat down and really faced one another with how we have changed, then a terrible chasm would open up between us, that if either of us were to make one big step towards the other they would fall into that chasm and be lost.

At any rate, I have reached the end-point of this stage of my journey. Greek and other kinds of heroes undertook journeys in order to make some great quest, even if it were, like Odysseus, merely to return home. They made their journeys despite many diversions from their true path—they kept getting lost, obstacles were always being placed in their way. Of course, these obstacles also made the journey interesting to others.

A journey implies ultimately reaching some goal, moving on and experiencing the feeling of movement, while hopefully something will be sorted out by the end of the trip. But I have no solutions, only more questions. I cannot yet find an end to my personal story. Perhaps I have to change course, set sail in another direction, launch out on another journey.